FOOD TRUCK BUSINESS

THE PRACTICAL BEGINNERS GUIDE ON HOW TO START AND RUN YOUR OWN SUCCESSFUL FOOD TRUCK BUSINESS IN 2023, AVOIDING COMMON MISTAKES WITH A COMPLETE EASY TO FOLLOW STEP SYSTEM

Kyle Locklear

Kyle Locklear

About The Author

Kyle Locklear was born in Fayetteville, North Carolina. As a food lover, he always dreamed of achieving his financial freedom by cooking. But without any formal qualifications it was something he believed would remain forever as a dream.

However, the more years went by, the more disillusioned Kyle felt about working for others. So, when he read about the food truck market and how it had grown by 12% per year since 2012, Kyle felt there was still a chance to make his dreams come true.

Investing what little he had saved, he took one step at a time, enjoying the freedom of the road and the opportunity to work wherever he pleased.

Since 2014, Kyle has traveled from Florida to Maryland to Colorado and beyond, learning the ropes from the food truckers he met along the way and earning money he never thought possible thanks to their advice.

Because of this accelerated growth path, in 2017 Kyle felt he had gained enough money and experience to take the leap: create a fleet of food trucks and go from food trucker to entrepreneur. And he did it.

Now Kyle has a fleet of 6 trucks, is a successful entrepreneur, and with the money earned from this business he has started new ones.

But Kyle remembers clearly where he came from and that he owes much of what he has today to the advice received from the more experienced colleagues he met on his journeys.

For this reason, now he wants to give back some of what he received, helping those with his same passion realize their dream by sharing with them the secrets of his success.

Through his food truck guide, in fact, Kyle shows how others can succeed in this business and live a life of freedom, both physically and financially, literally taking you wherever the road goes.

Table of Contents

Chapter 1. Introduction

Not too long ago, you had to look carefully or you'd miss it. If you were lucky, you could find one hanging out at the local corner shop. Weekends were usually a little easier. With so many people out and about, it didn't take too much effort to find what you were looking for.

Usually, you'd know you were close by taking a deep whiff of the air. The scents would just linger on the breeze. You'd inch closer and closer, salivating as the excitement grew, and you'd know you were so close to satisfying all of those urges.

And the waiting was terrible. This happened so rarely, and it was such an event, that you'd bounce restlessly, the change in your pocket jingling as you impatiently shifted from foot to foot, willing your favorite dish to still be available once you got to the front of the line.

But wasn't the payoff so very, very sweet? Wrapping your hands around that steaming hot delectable dish that you could only buy at your favorite food truck has always been a rewarding experience for the senses, the emotions, and, of course, the appetite.

Today, it's much easier to find a food truck. No longer relegated to corner shop parking lots or the street corners of weekend urban playgrounds, food trucks today pop up at small businesses, breweries or wineries, hardware stores, and even in larger neighborhoods. In fact, if you search online for "food trucks near me," chances are good that the nearest urban or suburban area will have quite a few options to try.

A food truck frenzy is quickly sweeping the nation, with new and exciting flavors appearing in communities all the time. There's no sign that this is a mere trend, either. Though it's impossible to know exactly how many food trucks are in service at any given time, reports indicate that there are around 25,000 food trucks in operation around the United States. And given two food trucks are rarely identical, even though they may serve the same dish, this means there are 25,000 exciting culinary adventures roaming the streets of this country just waiting to be discovered.

When it comes to food trucks we call it "opportunity" This word fits both the experience of the customers, who are given the opportunity to try new foods and flavors that might otherwise never have been known to them, and the food truck operator, who has the opportunity to share their favorite cuisine with their community.

The idea of "opportunity" resonates throughout the food truck community. There is, of course, the ability to earn a profit, to mobilize your business to attract the customers needed to keep your food truck afloat. A smaller-scale operation like a food truck gives restaurateurs a low-risk scenario in which they can try out new dishes and new concepts, as well. Plus, for those who love a good adventure, a traveling restaurant can provide an amazing way to interact with your community and beyond. You're only limited by how vast your dreams are, and how far your wheels can take you.

In this book, we'll explore the possibilities, potential, and realities of food trucks. We'll start with an introduction to the basics of food trucks. While some readers might be extremely familiar with the ins and outs of food trucks, some of you might be exploring this topic with a fresh eye. So, pull up a chair and we'll tuck into the history, the ideals, and the purpose of a food truck.

Once we've explored the evolution of the modern food truck, you should feel more inspired than ever to get your own model running. Therefore, we'll take a moment to look at how food trucks work. They are more than a truck with a microwave in the back. You might not have considered how to change the grease in a mobile fryer or how a refrigerator on a trailer keeps things cool. We'll investigate all of those details.

From there, we'll dive into making your food truck dreams come to life. By the end of this book, you should be comfortable creating a business plan for your future food truck, and have some good ideas about what to serve, how to serve it, and a few more ideas to help you drive off into the sunset with the food truck business you are so eager to create.

You will have a lot of work ahead of you, but the good news is that you can have your cake, or your tacos, noodles, smoothies...any type of cuisine you can dream of, and eat it too.

Since every food truck is unique—and every location may have different requirements—it wouldn't be possible or practical to include all the details that might be specific to your food truck and location. However, we've rounded up the resources you'll need to get those details.

Additionally, as much as I've tried to be "evergreen" in this book, laws, regulations, and permit requirements change frequently. This book will lean towards operating a food truck business in the United States, but food trucks are absolutely not limited to the U.S. In fact, food trucks are cultural icons in many parts of the world, and will likely have far different requirements and trends than in the US.

While this book is intended to be as inclusive as possible of various scenarios and dreams, always check with local resources to ensure you're meeting all of the necessary guidelines.

Just as you waited in line for what seemed like an eternity for that rare, delicious food truck treat, there will be a lot of patience and planning involved with your future food truck enterprise. However, just as that long queue paid off every time, so will this wait. With your new food truck come loads of opportunities, which can lead to a lifetime of new experiences.

Chapter 2. Introduction to Food Truck Industry: Data, Trends, and Stats

Strategy is a business's approach to grow the business, attract, and meet the needs of its customers, and compete effectively to improve the company's financial capacity. A company's strategy requires buy-in from employees in order to succinctly conduct business operations and meet targeted goals set by the business owner.

In this book, we'll talk about how to focus on developing your strategy to organize and operate your business and take advantage of the explosive growth of the food truck industry. There are still many underserved consumer markets ideal for mobile food units to fulfill.

First: Define your vision. Vision embodies the purpose of why your business exists and the need it will fill for the consumer.

Sell a product of convenience: A product's subjective value is more valuable to different people depending on how much they need or desire the the product.

The menu offering your mobile food unit serves can't be easily replicated by the consumer. In essence, the customer would rather purchase your product because it takes too much time to replicate in their own kitchen.

<u>Build your team</u>: The make-up of your team must complement the business tasks required to operate your mobile food unit efficiently and effectively. The tasks must fit the capabilities of the employee. You wouldn't hire someone with a speech impediment to serve as your cashier? This individual may be better suited to serve as the grill operator instead. Hire the right person to fill a vacant slot on your team!

<u>Product delivery</u>: In order to meet the consumer need for convenience, your business must have the capacity to meet product demand quicker than your competitor without sacrificing quality. Just good enough will not work, it must be near perfect. Your truck, commissary, and supply chain have to be organized to meet the consumer demand.

For example, I was one of 18 select vendors accepted to participate in a festival event with a projected one-day attendance of 40,000 patrons. In order to be accepted to this event, each vendor was required to have the serving capacity of 1,500-3,000 food or beverage items. The collective sum of each vendor was a hedge by the Event Coordinator to efficiently meet the consumer demand for this 6-hour event.

My small 6' x 10' mobile food unit was not capable of meeting the minimum serving capacity without being modified. Although, our food unit is fully equipped with a kitchen layout capable of competing with most brick-and-mortar restaurants, our unit could only handle 800 patrons a day independently. So, I developed a strategy to extend our work area to interact with customers and quickly fill food orders.

We placed a 12' x 12' canopy in front of our trailer, which served as our serving counter and storage area. The inside of the trailer was used exclusively to process food orders as tickets were received. This simple modification enabled us to effectively meet consumer demand. In fact, a food truck peer shared he was impressed with how efficiently we met demand in comparison to other vendors.

We processed customer orders in 8-minutes or less, this speed of efficiency resulted in our lines being shorter than peer food vendors; thereby, enticing other consumers to order from our food trailer instead. As you will read further in the book, American's hate standing in long-lines. *Speed of efficiency is a huge competitive advantage in the food truck industry.*

Consistency: Once you have perfected your recipes and menu offerings don't get complacent or lazy in the delivery of your product. Remain innovative in making things better, but do not cut quality over cheap substandard ingredients.

Maximize sales: Analyze your sales after every event. POS Systems provide statistics on what items were your best profit drivers; eliminate slow-selling items to better maximize your time and reduce waste. Immerse yourself in understanding the principles of improving your business operation and where to focus time and resources.

Best practices: If you intend to participate in the food industry, look at organizations that employ outstanding practices of performing tasks on a consistent basis. This is known as Benchmarking, the art of analyzing a leading company's performance in a particular function and adapting these practices into your business operation.

The best example of this discussion topic is in the movie called 'The Founder (2016), starring the actor Michael Keaton, playing the role of Ray Kroc. In the movie, the salesman Ray Kroc was astonished at how fast the fast-food eatery McDonald's® was capable of processing food orders so quickly. The McDonald's brothers, Richard McDonald and Maurice McDonald, invited Ray Kroc behind the scenes to observe the intellectual business process the McDonald brothers implemented to deliver their product to the customer quickly and consistently.

Best practices for use in the food truck industry don't necessarily have to come from the same industry, any business field that has outstanding practices is fair game for consideration.

Business legal structure: Organize your business structure to protect you and operate your business in a manner to not get sued. Why? Because when a lawsuit takes place, the government gets a third, the lawyers get a third, and your business gets overwhelmed because you have to worry about things other than running your business. Always conduct your business lawfully and honestly.

Exit strategy: Have an exit strategy. If you develop your business with a long-term growth strategy in mind, someone will come along and offer you a price to buy it. The food truck industry is just like most business industries, it is operating on a life-cycle that has yet to reach its peak core capacity—meaning there's a lot of growth still left in it.

Strategic Opportunities

The food truck industry is best equipped to meet consumer food needs that are not being met effectively by existing businesses, these consumer needs include:

- The underserved Vegan consumer market.
- Consumer diets sensitive to food allergens like nuts, dairy, and soy.
- The growing number of gluten food intolerant consumers with Celiac Disease.
- The small-scale operating aspects of a mobile food unit are ideal to meet these underserved consumer markets.

Executing your strategy may include:

- Pursuing opportunities to leverage with existing larger food establishments. Convey to the larger businesses how your small competitive advantage will enable the business to reduce their cost by leveraging your operation to outcompete larger food establishment rivals.
- Venturing into new customer markets by setting up your mobile food unit in new geographical areas (i.e., small towns or high school concessions).
- Out-innovating competing food trucks by exploring new menu product offerings or implement a food delivery service for offices during lunch operating hours.

Team Strategy Execution

- Build your team with the competencies, strengths, and capacity to execute your business strategy.
- Educate and convincingly communicate the business strategy to your team to obtain buy-in and allow your team members to execute their strategic roles.

Chapter 3. 9 Reasons Why You Should Open a Food Truck Business

The street food development has picked up fame in the course of the most recent couple of years, and if you've eaten from one recently, you will understand why. Street food is delightful, (typically) modest, and helpful for the client. TV is also contributing to this success with programming highlighting road merchants in The Great Food Truck Race On air on the Food Network. If you are interested in this book, you are probably keen on getting involved by beginning a mobile food business of your own. So, we should investigate the main reasons why starting a 'roach coach' can be a brilliant and remunerating adventure!

Have excitement, fun, and a whole lot of road to cover and sell enthralling dishes. The idea of a food truck business is a daring one, and there are lots of benefits in starting one. Listed below are the few benefits that pop up while thinking about it:

Maneuverable on Wheels

The most vital and common benefit that comes from owning a business on wheels is maneuverability. You can travel around the country and experiment with different sites and events to put up your food truck. The best part is that whenever you decide to move, you need not "carry" all your kitchen equipment; you just have to drive with it.

Fast and Moving

Apart from maneuverability, the food truck business offers you the ability to pick up your own pace. It has all the recipes to start up a serving and dining scenario quickly. All you have to do is to drive to the desired destination and open it up for serving. With a fast and efficient moving business, you will have all the time to do the things you wanted to do—bohemian style, with a touch of class.

Cool Factor with the Taste of Assured Profit

The changes and alterations you do to your vintage van to turn it into a charming food truck is itself a perfect alluring factor to draw in curious customers. People will be ready to pay up and find out what you are offering. A cooler-looking vehicle will attract more clients who want to station your mobile pantry for service at their events. It is also a great way of investment.

Freedom to Play with the Menu

You will always have the complete freedom to change and alter the menu according to the seasonal and regional demands. Moving from place to place, you will have the versatile option of selecting from various kinds of dishes you want to serve. The refreshingly new form of business with a changing menu will bring in more customers along with the regular ones.

The Comfort of Parking Anywhere You Want to

You need not to worry if the customers do not come to you. With a food truck in the hold, you can drive to a busy place and start selling in an instant to a crowd. Limits are indeed low in putting up this kind of food truck. You can even put one in front of busy bars, restaurants, and retail outlets. By this, you do no harm to their business, and you can attract more people in the locality and help the ones around you along the way.

Compact Simple and Efficient Kitchen

A large kitchen is always hard to manage. Your staff will find it easier to handle the small kitchen, and he/she will be efficient in doing his/her work. Pay for your staff will also be less as they are handling a small kitchen rather than big ones.

Apart from the service, the food truck business provides similar experiences that people have in a regular restaurant. But the whole prospect of selling and buying from a mobile pantry unit is itself exciting, and this will bring in lots of benefits than you can imagine. If your dream is to cater to the hungry folks around the country in a refreshingly new way, the food truck business is apt for you to enter and have fun. Do not worry about the benefits because you are assured of getting loads of it when you are in it.

A Truck Can Go to Where the Clients Are

This may not appear that enormous of an arrangement; however, it's perhaps the greatest advantage to operating a food truck. Generally, customary cafés can only service residents that are in the encompassing zone. Accordingly, it turns out to be subject to that individual community. Moreover, there are ordinarily numerous other cafés in that same territory to contend with. With a mobile food business, you are not constrained to one neighborhood; you can hit a wide range of various regions; you can set up at community occasions, like sporting events or festivals; attend outdoor foodie occasions; or set up late-night outside of night clubs and bars. Basically, it offers you much greater flexibility as far as locations and times where you can offer food to clients.

Compared to an Independent Restaurant Overhead Expenses Are Much Lower

It is considerably less costly to set up a food truck versus setting up a new café/restaurant and all the related costs that accompany—for instance, lease, build-out, and operating expenses. Since you are regularly paying for more workers and a physical structure, your overhead costs are just that much higher.

Serving Extraordinary Food that Makes Clients Happy Will Bring a Grin to Your Face

This is maybe the most significant part of running this sort of business. A decent mobile food business can profit around $75-150,000 per year, not a huge amount of cash. But if you are serving food around an idea and menu that you have endeavored to create and truly have faith in while building relationships with the community around you, it will make the endeavor all worthwhile. Likewise, food trucks are ready for advertising via social media. The demographic of clients tends to be a more youthful, urban crowd, who are very much associated through social media. Building a loyal following through promoting and branding utilizing Facebook and Twitter is free and fun. Food trucks have been a continuous pattern for quite a long while on both the east coast and west coast (and west coast specifically because of their atmosphere), but the two coasts have garnered a youthful and dynamic crowd that have embraced food truck and road food contributions as one of a kind, trendy, and vogue.

Chapter 4. The Best Way to Start A Successful Food Truck In 3 Steps

You have read about the awesomeness and benefits of putting up a food truck business. It is time to get on track and get to know about the factors and techniques to put up one. You must obviously know the basic essentials necessary in setting up a shop as such.

How to Build a Strong Business Plan

In order to succeed, you should have a pretty backed up plan for your business. You should know how to put an effective commercial plan when it comes to this type of business. There should be a decent clarity in what you want to do and how you want to do it.

Summary of business: This will be the brief proposal of your commercial plan to target the audience. You should know what you will be serving, where you are going to serve it and why it will be amazing in the area that you have chosen. You should also look past the present and see the big picture of your future in this business. You should be sure about the plan and you should plan accordingly if you want to reproduce the same idea with several food trucks all over the country in the upcoming years.

Description of the company: This is the vital part of bringing up any business and making it a "brand." You will have to give a description of the type of food truck that you intend to own, along with all the know-about of the competing restaurants nearby. You should also know how the food items in your menu would overcome and beat the competition out of the place.

Analysis of market: It is also an important part of the plan and it will be solely based on the extent to which you research the specific market. This type of analysis is essential in understanding the strategies that can be followed to get a hold of the market that you are getting into. When getting into a mobile food truck industry, these are the key points that should be duly covered:

- Current trends, growth rate and consumer data in the food industry.
- Age group, geography of the area, socioeconomic factors, and other demographic information of the audience in target.
- Need of the market and any specific seasonal or regional trends that might affect the market.
- Structure of pricing, total margin levels and other financial information.
- List of potential customers and how to gain their confidence in the present situation and in the future.
- Hurdles and problems in setting up the joint.
- Knowledge about regulations, such as food codes that have to be complied with, and how you would work to meet the requirements.

Organization and management: If you have only two people to work on the food truck of yours, it might not seem important to go into detail with organization and management. But it does not work like that. You have to be sure to provide the roles and responsibilities of each people who will be working with you. It is just to avoid confusions that might arise when business progresses. Everything including salaries and benefits, along with opportunities for growth are critical things to think about. The legal structure of the company or business should be clear. If you have associates, you should hold a partnership with their names, along with the percentage of their hold in the company. Also, you must know detailed information about the employees including educational background, preceding employment, and experience.

The final part of the plan is the product line. This is where you have to put in all the research information and merge it with the dreams of your personal level to meet what you wanted to deliver to your customers. You should be clear on what to serve and how you want to serve it when you reach this part of the business plan. With a great business plan to start and run a food truck, you will get a clear view of things to do further.

Business Plan Template

Now it is time to fund this business of yours and find the ways to acquire the adequate resource to put the food truck business up and running.

To successfully establish a food truck, you must have a clear vision of your product, the target market, and how you plan to differentiate yourself in the marketplace.

The following is an example of a business plan template for a food truck:

This business concept is for x-treme eats, a local food truck that sells delicious pizza Saturdays at King Park in the Historic District from 3:00PM - 6:00PM. Our catering service will also be available during all inclement weather.

Our value proposition is that we will provide the best-tasting pizza on the street for an affordable price. We will use social media to drive foot traffic, and our website to generate online sales. You will use the funds raised during this campaign to purchase a food truck, inventory, and marketing material.

Since restaurants are service-dependent, large amounts of fixed overhead are required in order to gain profits. We aim to cut out those expenses while maintaining the quality of our food through a food truck. Our target market is anyone who loves pizza and lives near Downtown Raleigh or King Park. Our primary method of marketing is through Facebook and Twitter, while using our website as an extra touchpoint for contacting customers or sending news about specials for your mobile phone.

In order to support our growth and prove demand for a mobile food service, we will begin by gaining permission from the City of Raleigh to operate our food truck in King Park. Once we have this permission, we will begin selling our pizza on Saturdays during the summer. We plan to report any profits or losses on a monthly basis in order to track our progress and make adjustments when needed.

In the event that our mobile business isn't successful, we have two alternate plans:

1. Open a brick-and-mortar store selling x-treme eats pizza. This would entail purchasing a place with adequate space for storing ingredients and making pizzas along with seating for dining in or taking out.
2. Sell our pizzas wholesale to local restaurants.

The first step to achieving our vision for x-treme eats is to raise $10,000. With this amount, we could purchase a used food truck and all the required permits in order to sell our pizza in King Park on Saturdays this summer. Our operation will remain mobile until we are profitable enough to build a physical retail location or until there is an increase in demand for delivery or carryout service that our food truck cannot meet.

Once we have raised our $10,000 goal then we can execute the following steps:

1. Raise additional funds for purchasing inventory such as cheese, toppings, and dough plus operational capital (e.g., equipment).
2. Purchase a food truck that meets all of the requirements for operating in King Park.
3. Draft up our menu and prices.
4. Purchase all of our inventory.
5. Decide upon a delivery radius and begin delivering pizzas once we have enough customers. The radius will either be restricted to the Historic District or expanded to include

other neighborhoods based on demand. (More deliveries will mean more income per hour, but it also means more gas costs). This step may be unnecessary if we decide to open a brick-and-mortar store instead of operating as a mobile business.

6. Develop a social media campaign that will spread the word about our food truck in advance of its opening.
7. Order all our plates, cups, utensils, napkins, and other items that we will need for service.
8. Buy a pizza oven to start baking our pizzas. Having a brick-and-mortar store would obviate this step.
9. Get insurance for the business. This will either be through our brick-and-mortar location or as a mobile business, depending on how we are operating at the time (mobile vs. physical).
10. Begin selling our pizza at King Park on Saturdays, weather permitting.

To measure our progress, we could use the following metrics:

- Customer feedback gathered from channels such as email, social media, and site reviews. We will be using this information to make improvements to our product and customer service. For example, if we receive a lot of bad reviews about delivery times or bad pizzas then we will reevaluate our delivery radius or find solutions for improving productivity (e.g., hire new drivers or order a new car).

- Number of visitors to our website or Facebook page. This metric will allow us to track interest in our product and gauge the effectiveness of our social media campaigns. It will also show growth in sales if we eventually open a brick-and-mortar store.
- Daily or weekly sales of products. This metric will help us determine if we are making enough money to pay for overhead and support growth.
- Monthly profits, losses, or break-even status. With this information we could determine whether we need to make changes to our business strategy, such as with our delivery radius or prices.

If successful, we will expand to operate at other public parks or downtown venues, such as Moore Square. This will allow us to reach a wider audience and increase our sales. We also intend on giving back to the community through donations of our proceeds to local charities, or in-kind donations of pizzas by helping with events and festivals that are hosted by local businesses or organizations. Finally, once we have established ourselves as a respected food truck and business, then we can begin the process of licensing and certifying our product for sale at grocery stores, convenience stores, and restaurants.

Raise Capital

Ways to raise the capital to kick start the business:

Crowdfunding is the best social and effective approach to choose if you want to run an interesting and charming business.

With little contributions from many people, the money that adds up will be enough to start one without a fuss. Thing about crowdfunding is the love involved in setting up the business.

You can always repay them back with invaluable discounts and free desserts.

There is another option of choosing a traditional bank loan. This is the most common choice taken by business owners in setting up their business. This is hard to get and you need to have a sufficient value of assets to gain the confidence of the bank in investing. Patience is very important in opting this way of raising capital. You have to live through the boring phase of extended approval process and things like that. However, the advantage is that interest rates are low.

If you are confident enough with a daring dream, you can opt to start with your own personal savings. If you don't want to be in debt, then this is the perfect way to start this business. It is a huge risk to take from your part and it is not a good idea if you don't have any extra money to invest later.

In credit union loans, the interest is based on the balance of the loan. If you pay a great amount of money towards the loan you have taken, your interest rates will dip effectively. This is a great idea to have when you are confident to turn over a huge profit at the beginning of the business.

Credit cards can also help you in setting up your own business. You can apply for the maximum number of credit cards and get the cash required to start the business. This is a daring option to take and you should be able to pay the money back at the correct time.

Friends and family will support you and your dreams for a long time to come. They will also be ready to go to the extent of financing it. But you should be careful when you take a loan from them because things can get messy and you might end up as foes. Even if it is a close friend or family, make sure that everything about the loan is on paper.

Licenses and Permits

Now as you are ready to put the idea of business up and running, you need to put together the information about licenses and permits essential to run the business.

- Tax registration: You should first get the Employer Identification Number (EIN) along with the application for tax-specific identification numbers in their states.
- Business licenses: You should apply for a Food Service Establishment Permit along with other licenses for the state.
- Local Permits: Along with the state permits, you will need various local permits. Each city and town will have different ways and process to get these permits. Few of the common permits that are necessary are: Alarm Permit, Health Permit, Signage Permit, Business License and Tax Permit and Zoning Permit.
- Filing of incorporators: If you are not the single owner of your business, you will need to register it as a legal entity.

A food truck business is an adventurous business to take on and it is not advisable to put all your personal assets in the line. Things can go wrong and it is ideal to have a partner to work things out with.

- DBA filing: In some cases, you should register yourself as Doing Business As, in which you have to legally give a name that your truck is running under.
- Documentation: You should be sure that the employees that you hire are allowed to work legally in the U.S. Assure that all the employees you hire will have to fill out an I-9 along with W-4 which collects the facts and documents to prove that the person can work legally. The most recent versions of these forms can be found in the IRS and you can use the government's E-Verify website to help with the I-9 form. After the hiring of an employee, you must report him/her to the state's directory within 20 days.
- Insurance and permits: Your employees should be covered with 2 key types of insurance: one is unemployment insurance and workers' compensation insurance. The former covers the employees in case you terminate them in which you have to pay the state for coverage. The latter covers the employee if they are harmed or injured while working. The state laws vary from state to state and it is advisable to ask your insurance agent or broker for help.
- Posters: If you are business owner with employees, you will be asked to display certain posters in the area where the employees can see them while working. It will have all the information in regards to their compensation and minimum wage.

- Food truck laws: Along with all these permits and licenses, you might also find that each state, town, and city might have their own laws in accordance with food trucks. If you are planning to drive along and operate in many areas, you will have to find separate licenses and permits for each one. Find all the information from the Department of Health. Also, try to find if there are any food truck associations in the city. They spend a lot of time and money to get good information about local laws and restrictions. You will also be able to connect with food truck owners who can help you in setting up a place to cook and serve.

Chapter 5. How To Avoid The Top 5 Causes Of Food Truck Failure

The food truck business is, indeed, a lucrative one, especially if it is run in an area where people buy food all the time.

Since its inception, the food truck business has continued to grow around the world, serving people who prefer not to cook or to take a break from cooking.

While the food truck business is a way to make money in this modern time, there are still a few shortcomings and mistakes which can pull your business down the drain.

Here, we have compiled some mistakes to avoid while running your food truck business:

1. Not setting your territory well

Customers are the backbone of a successful food truck business. This is why every food truck owner must set his vehicle in an area flooded with potential customers.

Meanwhile, a very good marketing plan will go a long way in aiding you to recognize potential customers, their homes, and the workplace.

Colleges, campuses, and street carnivals are other areas you can explore with your food truck.

2. Not choosing the right size truck

In as much as you may be planning to save money, buying a small truck for your food business could be detrimental for you and your employees, because they will be forced to work in a crowded and small place.

As a result, it is likely to affect how best your customers are served. Also, keep in mind that buying a big truck, which is costly, could be a wrong decision, especially if you have other important pending items you need money to get.

A good business plan will save you all the stress of making the wrong choice of buying a large or small truck.

3. Not welcoming or appreciating your customers

Top-notch customer service should always be your leading priority. Asides from providing quality food, customers are also watchful of how they are being treated.

If you fail to appreciate or welcome them well, you may not likely see them the next day. On the flip side, if they are appreciated and welcomed well, they will continue to flood your food truck every single day.

4. Not keeping the surrounding of your food truck clean

Keeping the surrounding of your food truck clean is crucial for a successful business. Your customers will not like to buy food where the environment or the food itself is not clean.

On their end, they will consider their health and overall well-being. So, a dirty food truck environment will only push your customers away, thereby, making you lose money.

5. Not having a social media presence

As the world is a global village, there is every need to place your food truck business online.

Social media is the best place to spread the fame of your business and draw potential customers.

For a start, you can have a Facebook page, IG page, Twitter, and a website. On some occasions, you can post the activities that go on in your food truck and share it for people to see.

If they are pleased with what they have seen, they will surely visit your food truck to patronize you.

Chapter 6. Why Social Media Is Crucial in the Food Truck Business

Let's first get straight precisely with which are the social media we're talking about. I'll be covering three in the following section:

Twitter

The Twitter revolution has always shown signs of change in the scene of mobile businesses and how they interact with customers. The steady stream, forward and backward, of little "tweets" among customer's and their favorite trucks, makes a superb close dialog through which the two sides enormously benefit. A decent food truck administrator doesn't deliver an address on his items; he makes conversation, which prompts the customer's constantly understand what is being offered and what its true value is.

It's also important for food truck owners to understand that Twitter provides not just an opportunity to share their location and menu, yet in addition to share exciting stories, jokes and begin engaging conversations revolving around food. Customer's hunger for a decent ongoing dialog and will re-tweet for quite a long time as more individuals voice their opinion and offer related anecdotes.

Here's a suggestion: Go on Twitter, transfer the name of a particular truck you'd like to follow, and join in the conversations. When you feel you've gotten a decent handle on the most proficient method to adequately "tweet," remember the following tips.

1. Have a methodology and stick to it. Stay consistent in the style and sort of substance of your "tweets."
2. Follow your kindred food truck administrators. There is a lot of smart thoughts out there.
3. Stay in contact with your customers! This can't be focused on enough. Stay consistently before your customers by tweeting each day. Any fool can do the tweeting, simply sincere. Most times the best dialogs are made by responding to a tweet, not by posting your own.
4. To begin an account on Twitter, and not keep it new with your tweets, is like cooking a delicious dish, and not eating it. Stay with it!

Facebook

Facebook is additionally another incredible social media tool that can promote your food truck. Unlike Twitter, having a Facebook page enables you to go past minor words and instead post entertaining videos and short clips about your food truck. I think posting videos where you show viewers how you set up a portion of their favorite foods is an incredible idea. (I doubt I'm the one in particular who isn't even slightly interested in "watch us wash our food truck! So fun!" videos...)

If you have a website together with your Facebook account, link the two! On your website have an option to "click here" and be sent to the next page. This can increase web traffic for your food truck business. Additionally, don't neglect to use catchphrases that tie into your truck, cuisine, and location. Find the best watchwords and use them (An expression of caution: don't overdo it or you'll get blacklisted immediately).

Chapter 7. 5 Strong Social Media Strategies to Success in the Food Truck Business

Wordpress Is Not Just for Bloggers

Wordpress began as a platform for bloggers and remains as the most popular choice in this sector. WordPress began as a platform for bloggers and remains as the most popular choice in this sector. But there is more than blogging.

. Today, small businesses and even larger businesses use WordPress to power their websites.

Here are some actual food truck businesses that use WordPress to power their websites.

- Seoulful Philly - http://www.seoulfullphilly.com
- Purple People Eatery - http://www.purpleppleatery.com
- JapaCurry - http://japacurry.com
- Liba Falafel - http://libafalafel.com
- Barbed Wire Reef - http://www.barbedwirereef.com
- Wheels on Fire - http://wheelsonfirepizza.com
- Ladybird Food Truck - http://ladybirdfoodtruck.com

I hope you could check some of those sites out. It's possible that those food trucks had web designers create those sites for them; but even so, you can do it yourself. They all started out as templates and once you know how one works, you can figure out how to use almost any WordPress template. I always put it this way: if you know how to fill out web forms or create online Christmas cards, you should be able to figure out how to use WordPress.

In fact, you can check out WordPress yourself for no cost with templates and all! So, if you've never used WordPress before, this is where you should go to get a free website:

http://wordpress.com

Here you can get a free WordPress site up and running so you can experience first-hand how it all works before going the self-hosted route, which involves buying a domain hosting service. Creating a website on WordPress.com has one disadvantage though. Your web address will not be a simple name like just your food truck name. Say for example your truck is called the Heavy Burger. Your website URL would be:

https://heavyburger.wordpress.com

Notice the ".WordPress" text in the URL? This is the result of using the free version of WordPress for your website. This is entirely usable but not easy for your customers to remember. And it doesn't look as professional. I've seen many businesses and food trucks use this as their website. But this is not ideal, as you can imagine.

One way around this is to pay WordPress for additional services like having a custom domain name. This could be an alternative if you have already built out your website on WordPress.com and don't feel like rebuilding it again on your own hosting company.

By paying for premium services on WordPress.com, you can use a custom domain name (get rid of the .wordpress.com), have extra data storage and eliminate ads from your site.

Start with a Test Website

For a good start, you can first create a test website on Wordpress.com to experience firsthand how the interface works without it being live on your business website. It's really simple to do and all you need is an email address to get set up. I suggest using an alternate email address, as opposed to your main business email for this test account.

Get familiar with the different tabs and buttons. It should be pretty intuitive and it won't take you long to figure it out. Don't be afraid to click and try things because this is a test website so it doesn't matter what you do here.

This is a short list of the things you should do after you get signed up:

- Create a blog post
- Upload an image to your blog post
- Include a YouTube video on your blog post
- Upload your logo
- Search for WordPress themes
- Change the theme of your WordPress site
- Post a blog post

- Schedule a blog post
- Connect your Twitter or Facebook feed to your site
- Share your test posts on Facebook and Twitter

At this moment, those are some of the basic things you need to know when running your real WordPress website. If you can do all of the things listed, you will be able to run your own site with confidence. It really is pretty simple and even non-technical people can figure out how to use WordPress fluently.

Advanced WordPress Techniques

That's not all you can do with WordPress but in this book, I wanted to keep it simple and get you at least to set up the test account to get you moving forward. However, I will touch on some more advanced features of WordPress just so you are at least familiar with them.

One of the things that WordPress does well with is SEO or search engine optimization. What that means is that WordPress can help your website be found in search engines like Google, Bing and Yahoo. That is if you provide some parameters that are relevant to your website and what people are searching for. This is not a tutorial for SEO; but with a few keystrokes, you can greatly increase your website's chances of being found in a search.

Title Description and Tags

When you write a post, you are only required to have a title to go along with it. That's the easy part. Make sure your title tells the reader exactly what your post is about in a concise way. However, you have to be careful about the optional parts of your posting. That includes the description and tags.

When finishing your post, do not forget to fill out the fields for the description and tags. The description is obvious what it is but is limited in the number of characters that will be shown in a search result. The maximum limit is usually 160 characters. So, when writing your description, summarize your post in about 2 short sentences. It can be longer but the search engines won't read anything over 160 characters.

Tags are just keywords that are relevant to your posting. So, when you're done with your description, add some relevant tags or keywords to your post. These can be single words that are relevant to your post and help the search engines determine what your post is about. You don't have to think about this too much but you should be able to determine your keywords easily from your blog post.

SEO Suggestions

Food trucks are unique businesses and usually based in a single market or area. This is important to remember when adding tags and writing your description. You want people to find you by searching for the type of food you serve and the locations you operate in.

Let's imagine you have a food truck in Phoenix, Arizona called Big Daddy BBQ. Your menu has a several BBQ items that are popular.

People searching for restaurants might be searching for a certain type of BBQ so here are some examples of keywords to use with this fictional food truck business:

- Big Daddy BBQ
- BBQ pulled pork restaurant
- Authentic BBQ Phoenix
- Phoenix BBQ restaurant
- Phoenix food truck
- Scottsdale BBQ
- Best BBQ in Phoenix
- Southern BBQ
- BBQ catering Phoenix

I think you get the idea. The local emphasis is important because your main customers are in your hometown. Not every keyword has to have your city name in it but a couple of them should include the city name. It's the same in regards to your description. You should mention your city name in the description to make it more relevant in searches.

This is a simple description of how SEO works but if you can put some of this basic knowledge to work on your website, you will be miles ahead of the other food trucks that don't pay attention to this stuff! It is a little extra work but it really doesn't take up that much time in the grand scheme of things.

Chapter 8. Top 6 Marketing Ideas to Gain Customers for Your Food Truck

Offer Something for Free

Offering something small for free to each customer is a good way to ensure happy customers and to distinguish you from other trucks. It is also good for keeping people occupied. As the orders come piling in and the wait time becomes longer, giving people something small to snack on is a good way to keep them occupied until their food arrives. People can become impatient with the longer wait times but if they've already received something, they'll be more patient with you.

What to offer depends mainly on the type of food you propose but it is easy to give out free items that don't cost much. We've done homemade popcorn and homemade chips, as well as small desserts.

A bag of popcorn for each person waiting won't cost you much and the benefits will be a happier and more tolerant customer. I found that this is a nice way to get a friendlier and more loyal customer base, especially if you continually serve at a particular location.

Let the Order Line Be Longer than the Pickup Line

It may sound confusing, so I'll explain it better. If you have a large number of people waiting to order as well as people waiting for their food, it's a better idea to make the people looking to order wait than it is to let the people looking to pick up wait.

Once people have ordered, they're ready to take it and go; they get impatient very quickly. They only can think about their order has been received and they want it immediately, without thinking about all the other orders on the board. People waiting to order, on the other hand, are only impatient because there are people in front of them in-line and so their impatience lies more with the people ahead of them than it does with you.

With a long list of orders on the board, things will get stressful in the truck pretty quickly. You will want to take orders but also be scrambling to get food orders out the window. However, from experience, it's better to hold off on taking more orders if there's a large number already on the board to concentrate on.

Let the people waiting to order know that you are busy clearing the board and will be with them shortly and focus on getting some of the orders out to waiting customers. That way you will keep people's wait times for their food down, which is generally more important than the line waiting to order.

Offer Items from Your Catering Menu

Though this book doesn't focus on the catering side of your business, serving food on the street is a good chance to promote it. A good way to do this is to offer 1 or 2 items from your catering menu. Assuming you have a catering menu, a good way to land catering gigs is to choose a couple of items from this menu for street service.

Now maybe your catering food is more tailored towards cocktail parties and smaller foods but that's fine. You can offer them as a side, give some out for free or change the item to turn it more in a main dish and less of a smaller finger food type.

However, you do it, it's good to test out how people like the items you will be serving at your catering events. It will also be a good chance for people who may be planning a catering gig to get a taste of what they can expect if they book their gig with you.

If you make sure to promote it and make a note on your menu that the item is from your catering menu, it will let people know that you do cater and that this is the quality they can expect. So besides satisfying people's taste buds on the street, you will be subtly promoting your catering, which is where you can make very good money.

Assuming your food tastes great, this is a good way to attract people to your catering business and give people the idea of booking their gig with you.

Always Ask If They Would Like a Drink

This may sound painfully obvious but it's easy to forget. Especially if you are busy, you will be too focused on taking orders and getting food out the window and you may forget to ask each customer if they'd like a drink. In addition to putting drinks on the menu, it's a good idea to ask each person if they'd like to add a drink if they haven't already asked for one.

Every dollar counts and this is a good and effortless way to make a couple of extra bucks out of each order, which throughout a day of selling will start to add up. Again, you will want to price your food so that adding a drink can add to a number that goes with a bill. While you won't be able to implement this strategy in all cases, still try to keep it in mind.

For example, maybe your main item sells for $8. It isn't a stretch to ask 2 dollars for a can of Coke and most people won't think twice about handing you a 10-dollar bill. It's always a good idea as well to offer a discount if they include a drink with their meal or for a combo deal with a drink and a side.

Whatever you decide, be sure to ask every customer if they'd like to add a drink. A lot of people who wouldn't order one will end up getting one; you just have to put the idea in their head.

Advertise Your Menu on Social Media

This is important for several reasons. You will want your regular customers to know what you will be offering that day and hopefully, it's something they've had before and want to try again. It's also for people who haven't tried your truck. This is where a good menu is important, with great-sounding food. You will want those good descriptions to catch their eye and entice them to come and check your truck out.

I've found that it's rather boring just to write out what you are offering that day, especially if your main social media advertising is on hosts that are picture-based. This is where taking pictures of your food is important, as you can show them what you will be offering as well as describe it. This is where you will get people excited.

If they see what you are offering and it looks great, they'll be much more inclined to come to enjoy your food than if you were to just describe it. This can be done in many different posts, one for each item. That way you will give more people a chance to see your posts and they'll be able to see everything you are offering, hopefully enticing them to be excited about a number of your items.

In addition to pictures, add what each item consists of; just write the same description that's on your menu. The picture and description should be enough for people to want to come down and check it out. If your pictures look good and the description is intriguing, this shouldn't be difficult.

You should do this with your location: Throwing up a picture of what you will be serving and letting them know where and when they can enjoy it is a great way to combine these two. Do this when you know your location, throughout the week, and the day before and day of. That way you will build some anticipation and give more people a chance to see what they can hope to enjoy and how to get it.

Make Sure the Spot's Worth It

After spending all this time and money, you will want to make sure that, on average, you are making money. To turn a profit on a food truck it's not easy as it seems. There are so many factors that are working against you, most of which you can't control. It may sound like I'm being negative but the truth is, losses can begin to pile up quickly and as such it's important from the get-go to recognize this and do what you can to mitigate these losses.

Whether it be bad weather, a poor customer turnout, or just pure bad luck, you will want to identify quickly if the spot you've chosen is worth it. Often, you will return to the same spot many weeks in a row. This makes sense, as it's not easy to find spots to park your truck, whether that's because of city regulations or because there just aren't that many good places to sell food. Whatever it is, you will want to decide quickly whether the spot you find yourself at is a spot you should continue to attend.

In a lot of instances, good spots can end up costing money before you even show up. This will depend on your city, but sometimes your best bet is on private property and you will end up shelling over a reasonable amount of cash just for the right to sell there. This can be a minor expense if the spot is great; but if it isn't, you could find yourself at a loss at the end of the day.

Factoring in the fee to be there, food costs, truck costs, not to mention all the hours you put into making the food, you want to be turning a profit; and if you are not, odds are you should find a new spot. Often, focusing on all the other factors that go into running a food truck business is easy; but finding a good location, which is a big part of making money, is forgotten.

Be honest with yourself and if the spot sucks, don't keep showing up. Save that money you'd otherwise be wasting and find somewhere new where you can hope to establish a good customer base. It's better to review the plan, instead of keep throwing money at a venture that isn't profitable, especially at the early stages when you can't afford to waste money.

Proximity to similar vendors: When participating in festival events, ask the event organizer to not place you next to food vendors that sell the same entrée items you are selling. Meaning if BBQ Pulled Pork is on your menu and your neighboring food vendor is selling BBQ Pulled Pork, you are in direct competition with them. This can lead to confusion among prospective patrons and dwindle your sales.

Best location: As you plan to participate in various events, some food vendor applications will allow you to select where you prefer to setup. As a general rule of thumb, always select spots near the Beer Garden, Bathrooms, and ATMs. Why? Two words...*Foot Traffic.*

Foot Traffic is your best friend when participating in festival events. Being close to the Beer Garden, Bathrooms and ATMs provide prospective vendors with the greatest exposure to patrons attending festival events.

Chapter 9. Proven Strategies to Keep Your Business Profitable for The Long Run

What Numbers Should I Know?

"Know your numbers!" is a classic and overused phrase. However, it's vital to know your numbers—don't let the knowledge of them get away from you. Much stress and frustration can stem from the guessing game that ends up being played when you don't know your numbers.

You need to know how much money is coming in and going out every day, week, month, and year to know whether what you are doing is working. Knowing as much data as possible about your business will help take that guessing game off your plate and lighten the stress that comes with it.

The guessing game hurts you, your team, your business, and your customers. Once you know the basic numbers, you can start to dive in deeper. Then you can begin creating what I call "NextGen Numbers."

Later in this point, I have included an extensive list of definitions and formulas on how to figure out those numbers.

Time to go beyond just knowing your numbers. Let's put them to work!

If you have your numbers in a program, it should be easy to break them down so you can see month-over-month and yearly trends. Utilizing these trends will help you get out of the guessing game and into making educated decisions based on the cold hard numbers, not what you feel.

Too often, people fall back into going with their gut feelings and what they knew to be true at one point in time. Things are changing every single day—in life and in business. It's imperative that you stay on top of the mounting trends in your business to avoid any blindside hits.

You could utilize the data you collected to make investing in your business a lot simpler because you will know and not be guessing. Expanding and contracting areas of focus for your business will be leaps and bounds easier when you have the data laid out in front of you.

When was the last time you set sales goals for your business? You've heard that question before, I'm sure but I want you to take it one step further. Instead of simply saying that you want to hit X sales goals for a period, track it and give periodic updates to your team based on the data available. This way your crew can stay on task and on track to meet those goals. Tracking will also enable conversation on how to meet those goals. Without those conversations, you aren't giving your team a clear path to success, which is a quick way to wind up having unmet expectations and all-around disappointment.

Try to keep your goals obtainable and reasonable so you can use them as a springboard of encouragement for you and your team.

Small wins are wins. You don't have to swing for the fences for a home run every time you go to set goals. Increases and decreases of 5 to 10 percent over specific periods of time should be reasonable. Setting such reasonable goals will also help with combating big downturns if you land the business that is a one-and-done deal. Next, we can move on to creating your own NextGen Numbers.

How Can I Create NextGen Numbers?

NextGen Numbers can be set for every position in your business and are different in every industry. They will help you track inefficiencies, which will save you money and add profit to your bottom line.

One example of a NextGen Number I created and used was to track the accuracy of our stock pickers in our central warehouse. Every day, hundreds of parts were picked off our central warehouse shelves to be sent to our satellite stores for stock and specific orders. We used a scanner and barcode system to create orders for the satellite stores that in theory should have been 100 percent accurate. As we quickly found out, that was far from the case.

Some members of our warehouse team were much more accurate in their scanning than others. The day after the inventory was sent, we would receive the corrections back. From there, I kept a running tally in a spreadsheet that gave team members a percentage score on their accuracy individually and as a whole.

Based on this data, we determined we were able to lower our percentage of shipping errors out of our warehouse.

When you have to figure out what to track to base your NextGen Numbers on, you have to look at what data you have available to you. What data can you extract from the daily process you already have going on in your business? Once you decide what to track, you just need to keep a record of it in a spreadsheet. It doesn't need to be a super-complex spreadsheet but gather as many data points as possible to help you build an average and, most importantly, an expectation. Once you have that baseline of numbers, you can start to build an expectation and build predictions for how changes in your current process will affect the numbers. The results will most likely surprise you!

Once you have your basic numbers tracked and have goals built around them, you will be able to start finding and tracking these NextGen Numbers to start the process of building your business into a well-oiled machine.

Here's an outline of the basic numbers you should know to make educated decisions and help build your NextGen Numbers.

Expenses

Money spent in order to generate revenue.

Expense Target

The projected goal of the total expenses incurred during a specified time period.

Revenue

Income generated from sales.

Revenue Target

The projected goal of the total revenue during a specified time period.

Cost of Goods Sold

Cost of obtaining materials and creating the finished goods that are sold.

Formula: Beginning Merchandise Inventory + Net Purchases of Merchandise – Ending Merchandise Inventory

Profit

The surplus of money after total costs are deducted from total revenue.

Formula: (Revenue – Cost) / Revenue x 100

Profit Margin

Percentage of profit left after taxes.

Formula: After-Tax Profit x 100 / Cost of Sales

Net Profit

Total earned or lost in a specified time period. Formula: Total Expenses – Total Revenue

Gross Profit

Difference between revenue and cost of goods. Formula: Revenue – Total Expenses

Debt

Obligation to pay money.

Accounts Receivable

Number of sales not yet paid for by customers.

Accounts Payable

Unpaid bills.

Return on Investment (ROI)

A percentage that compares profitability or efficiency of investments.

Formula: (Net Profit / Total Investment) x 100

Stock Turnover

The number of times inventory is replenished during a specific period.

Formula: Cost of Sales / Average Inventory

Sales

While it can be talked about as revenue, you should also know the number of units sold and the average number of transactions in a given period.

Sales Closing Rate

Percentage of prospects who become paying customers.

Formula: (Number of Successful Sales / Number of Leads) x 100

Average Time to Collect

The medium amount of time it takes you to collect your accounts receivables.

Salaries

The amount you are paying your team members in specific roles.

Cost of Customer Acquisition

Amount of expenses in marketing to acquire one customer.

Formula: Marketing Expenses / Number of Customers Acquired

How Do I Increase My Profit?

Now that you have gone through all of your numbers and even created new numbers to help, we can look at balancing your sales mix and examining ways to plus-up your current offer.

First, look at what percentage is coming from high-profit margin versus low-profit margin sales.

Now, take a look at how much you are spending on high-profit margin sales versus low-profit margin sales. This comparison helps you estimate how you can better spend your money and create a game plan for injecting more high-profit margin sales into your mix. Allocating money for specific items in proportion to your overall budget will give insight into where to spend your capital to gain best outcomes.

Getting your mix right can include branching out into bringing more product lines together. You need to be careful, though, that you are not spending too much of your budget on betting whether a new product will take off with your customers. Identifying great add-on sale items that come with high-profit margins is the key to bolstering your overall profit margin. Have no fear in trying something new., but make sure you educate your team on the benefits of selling the new products. If you have their support and they are educated, you are increasing your new products' potential success.

Selling to existing customers is always much easier than finding new ones. Getting feedback from your customers on what they would like to get from your business is always helpful for making more informed decisions. You can achieve that feedback in many different ways from just straight out asking the right questions to giving out surveys. You will most likely get opinions from the happiest or unhappiest people, so you will need to set up the survey to give you an average response.

A very crucial part of the business plan would be the break-even analysis as well as the profit forecast. These two calculations will give you an insight into how you must run your business in the first few months of operations and give comfort to financers as to your ability to repay the debt. While we are on that subject, don't try to convince a financer to loan you money on a truck that is in poor condition. Either find something new or in excellent condition or get a quote to put the truck in top condition. Do not expect a bank or finance company to lend its money on a bad truck and don't even think about doing that yourself. This is not a place to shortcut.

Chapter 10. Secrets to Build Your Own Food Truck for Maximum Profit at Minimum Cost

How To Build The Best Food Truck At The Lowest Price

When recommending those venturing into the realm of the business of mobile food truck, I can't pressure enough the importance of building an "optimal" food truck. What's more, by optimal I don't mean the biggest, worst, most expensive new truck you can design only for its pure fun. You truly need to remember that you are building a food truck to yield maximum profits yet at a minimum cost, so you can look professional and be fruitful while keeping however much of those profits as could be expected for yourself and your family! When you dig in, you will find there can be quite a lot to it. I genuinely need to give you a few secrets right here that I believe are the most important considerations, which ought to be sufficient to guide you in the right direction.

Number one, I would unequivocally propose you go with a used food truck in good state. Furthermore, finding one is, in reality, entirely straightforward. A lot of industrial trucks are now built to work for 300,000, 400,000, or even 500,000 miles! The sweet spot is frequently found by acquiring something like a UPS or FedEx truck, a bread delivery truck, or even a potato chip delivery truck. These models are genuine work steeds, and you could likely bargain one with around 100k miles at a not too bad cost; hell, even 150,000 miles still factors in a lot of helpful work-life to begin and develop your mobile food business. Furthermore, guarantee the truck has been well maintained, which undoubtedly, was from FedEx, UPS, or any such big-name truck armada. You need to have it inspected by mechanic; yet this course will be your most economical option, and one that will work well for you because, again, these things last 300,000, 400,000, 500,000 miles easily.

When stocking your food truck, go for middle-of-the-line equipment that is going to be tough. What's more, I need to impart to you here specific ways to ensure yourself. I lost a considerable number of dollars since I didn't realize what to look for when I was constructing my mobile kitchen. Furthermore, although I did the exploration and went to five or six other truck builders, I still got exploited. Building the truck is here and there a bit like the Wild, Wild West. For reasons unknown, there's not a lot of regulation in this industry, and I don't know why. Something I will urge you to do to protect yourself is to sign a written contract and, when it involves an out-of-state vendor, make beyond any doubt that, if there is a dispute, the agreement states that it will be governed under the jurisdiction of your home state. Make sure the out-of-state seller comes to you if/regarding this. The other thing I would do is make sure to pay them in thirds. I mean a third after signing the agreement, a third midway finished when you can expect the vehicle and make beyond any doubt that it's coming along on timetable, and afterward the final third once you've examined your food truck and it's transported.

Furthermore, in further consideration when building your food truck for maximum profit at minimum cost, make beyond any doubt you go to your nearby jurisdiction and know their laws and codes first that have your truck built to those specs. Also, here's a reward tip for you. Write in the contract that the truck must be built to these codes and specifications, and if they are not, the seller will have to pay to have it revised. Don't attempt to work this out after the build; do it in advance the right way while you influence the builder. This is a big mistake I see numerous clients that I counsel will make. Sometimes it's past the point of no return when I get to them, yet I need to make beyond any doubt you don't make this mistake. Make beyond any doubt that you know the codes—and coincidentally, for each city or jurisdiction you're going to stop in, you need to go to their wellbeing division and learn what their codes and laws are. For example, Baltimore, where I worked for a long time, is one of the toughest in the nation. However, yours can fluctuate wildly in certain viewpoints.

What's more, you need to make beyond any doubt that your truck looks appealing. Keep in mind this is your mobile billboard, and it produces catering employments and new clients for your café.

How Do I Know I've Found the Best Food Truck Business?

Not every person who offers a feast in a hurry is in a similar class. To find the right portable food truck business, you need to do some examination. Do you need a concession business like the one on each other corner? Also, would you like to be the food concession that offers a crisp and one-of-a-kind menu that stands in a class independent from anyone else?

You start a new business for yourself since you need to turn a benefit. To do that, you need to choose your activity shrewdly. A decent portable food truck system will provide all the fundamental devices, assets, and guidance to guarantee that you escape the door rapidly and effectively. Giving this a shot your very own will prompt many stumbles and wrong turns. Do you believe you have room schedule-wise and cash to hazard going only it? So before settling on anything, find an industry leader who has a training program set up and systems intended to spare you long periods of experimentation.

The best versatile food businesses have a demonstrated business model that is constructed and intended to pull in customers from a large fragment of the populace. They provide you with training from the day you consent to your Franchise Arrangement and support for as much as you are in business.

Where lunch customers once needed to agree to solidified level, boring burgers, solidified fries and sandwiches with a couple of choices, the best versatile food concessions offered hand-tapped Vermont meat burgers and healthy options, for example, an assortment of new wraps. They have developed exponentially every year and keep on outperforming desires even in a horrid economy.

When you choose to band together with the top versatile concession establishments, you will maintain a portable food business with heart. You and your staff will have an extraordinary time serving customers with a full menu of exciting and healthy choices. Furthermore, when you're working in a kept space, there's no space for error. Your training gives all of you the plans and food preparation protocols that you have to draw in your customer base and surpass their desires every single visit. What's more, their best-in-class electronic announcing systems and back-office support mean you never need to manage long stretches of desk work

Why to Buy A Mobile Food Concession Business

The concession business is quick turning into a popular way to make a living in the restaurant industry. There are a few reasons to go into this type of business before you attempt to start a stationary restaurant. Initially, starting a versatile concession business is a much smaller investment to take. Secondly, you can make a name for yourself in the local community. Lastly, as the business will be mobile, you could attempt different types of locations before choosing only one. In the wake of opening your own food concession business, you may decide to keep it for all time, start a restaurant notwithstanding it, or change easily into the eating establishment you always longed for owning.

The principal reason to choose to run a versatile food concession business before a block-and-mortar restaurant is that it is a lot of smaller monetary risk and weight to take on your shoulders. If you are a newcomer in the food industry, the risk in acquiring a stationary business is higher. If operating a restaurant is something you always needed to do, this is an extraordinary way to start small and to stir your way up to the position you want. This type of business is small and a lot easier to maintain and to run than merely bouncing into a 75 fixed-location restaurant. A concession trailer or food truck can mean a large number of dollars to invest, while a conventional eating establishment can represent a larger amount of dollars, and that's only the tip of the iceberg. Along these lines, being practical: if your business fails, you will have spent less money.

Another reason to sell food from a concession trailer initially is that you can feel free to establish a company name in the local community. If you don't have the funds immediately to put into a restaurant, the concession trailer can be the method by which you acquire those funds. At the same time, you are working up benefits and offering to the locals, and you're making your name and your story known to people. If you have more standard clients than another restaurant with a similar name as your concession business, you will almost certainly attract customers while never having opened the customary restaurant.

Lastly, one more reason to start a food truck concession is that since the business is mobile, you can move to a new location if the one you're in isn't effective. Much of the time with conventional restaurants, you get into a place that, out of the blue, there is not great business. You may have every one of the segments a decent restaurant needs: a great neighborhood, a lot of pedestrian activity, and incredible food and administration; regardless, it doesn't acquire the salary you figure it should. Sadly, with a fixed restaurant, there isn't much you can perform aside from sticking it out or surrender. In any case, one of the particular preferences of a versatile truck or trailer is you can go anywhere the money is; you need to locate that ideal spot.

Owning a restaurant is a fantasy for some people, yet it isn't always open. A lot easier, less expensive, and progressively helpful way to get your feet wet in the industry is to start your very own food concession business. These and different reasons give verification that starting the smaller investment of a concession trailer can be a clever thought.

There are a few reasons to choose a versatile food business over a conventional stationary restaurant. It is a less expensive investment, you can establish a name for yourself, and you can likewise move your business to another location if it isn't profiting according to your initial expectations.

Chapter 11. Tips for Buying a Second-Hand Food Truck

Buying a second-hand truck is one way to get your business up and running with limited investment. Before purchasing a food truck, you must consider many factors, not least of which is cost. Here you can find some tips in how to buy a second-hand food truck so that you can avoid costly mistakes.

First, you have to know what you are looking for. Do not rely on the seller to tell you everything about the truck. He might be biased towards it and will only look at the positive side of his product. Inspect the truck based on your own criteria.

Here are few ways to inspect a second-hand food truck:

- Check for any damages like cracks in the frame and body, rusts in the metal, and missing parts like doors or panels. Make a list of these things. Hire a mechanic to inspect for any engine problems that were not visible when buying. He will also check for any mechanical problems that might cause expensive repairs in future such as brakes or air conditioner leakage among others.
- Check the electrical system. Make sure that everything works and there is no sign of damage or wear and tear. This will allow you to save up a lot of money in repair in the future because you can fix most of the problems before they develop into something larger.

- Check the fuel tank for rust, damages, or cracks. You should buy a truck with a fuel tank that is free from rust because it can be very expensive to replace it later on. A new tank will cost you around $1,000 while second-hand tanks will go for around $700-$800.
- Check all the equipment inside like coolers, stoves, microwaves, espresso machines and sinks to see how well they function. Check the forks, knives, spoons, and other utensils to see that they are clean and free from rust or cracks. Replace anything that is cracked or damaged.
- Check the generator for any cracks, missing parts or signs of wear and tear. You can run generators for an average of 3-4 years before they stop working. But if you will be running it for more than 4 years, you might consider replacing it with a new one in order to avoid future complications.
- Check lights inside and outside the truck including the fans, ceiling lights and door lights. They should all work properly without any sign of damage or wear and tear.
- Check the water system and drains for any sign of leaks. You don't want to buy a truck full of water leak because this can cause damage to your food and it might be a health hazard, too.
- Check the paint inside and outside the truck for any rust or cracks. If there are none, you can repaint your truck. A second-hand food truck with no rust or cracks on the paint will save you a lot of money in repainting job in the future.
- Check for tools like screwdrivers, sockets, wrenches, pliers, and hammers to see if they are all in good condition.

Replace anything with noticeable wear and tear or damage because they are important when working on trucks.

- Check for tables, chairs and stools that are inside the truck. They should be in good condition because they can cause accidents if they are broken or missing.

After you have inspected the truck, you will know what to consider when buying a second-hand food truck.

Secondly, other than inspecting the truck, you must also find out how much it is worth. You will need this information during negotiation when buying it from the owner. Here are few ways you can find out the value of a truck:

- Search for any food truck for sale listings online or in classified ads. See what others are selling their trucks for and then consider whether your truck is in good condition or not.
- Check the blue book value for trucks of the same make and model as yours to find out if it's higher or lower than you think you should ask for your own truck. Remember that a second-hand food truck costs more than other trucks because of its size, additional equipment, and its importance in bringing delicious meals to people.
- Check the price of new trucks of the same make and model that you are considering buying. If the price is lower than your target price, you should buy a new truck instead.
- Check for opinions about your desired truck on websites or blogs. They can give you a reasonably good idea about how much to pay for it.

- Finally, when buying a second-hand food truck, do not forget to get repair estimates from trusted mechanics before engaging in negotiations with the seller, because second-hand trucks generally have problems that must be fixed before using. When getting estimates, tell them that you are planning to use the truck for commercial purpose, so they won't ask you to pay an arm and leg for minor repairs or maintenance jobs like oil change and tire rotation.

Chapter 12. Food Safety for Food Truck

Food safety will be your constant companion when your food truck is up and running. You will need to abide by all the relevant laws and the inspections that accompany them. If you're serious about your business, you'll prioritize food safety above all else. It's just good business. You don't want to be the food truck where people get poisoned.

Many restaurant owners adopt an antagonistic stance against food safety inspectors. This is completely pointless. The inspector isn't there to shut you down. They're simply there to ensure that hygiene is being maintained and that you're not compromising the safety of your employees and customers. They gain nothing by shutting you down so always strive to maintain the highest standards of food safety in your kitchen.

Check with the local health department to identify the frequency of food safety inspections. They usually occur once every year but you never know when a surprise inspection might occur. While local officials have health codes, the Food and Drug Administration (FDA) has its own set of guidelines. These are also enforced by local health department officials. The latest version of the FDA health codes can be found at https://www.fda.gov/media/87140/download.

Passing Inspections

Passing inspections is important, but don't adopt the attitude that they're an exam you need to prepare for. Instead, understand that they're in place to protect you. If a customer of yours becomes ill, they may sue you in court. Do you really want to expose yourself to such processes? Think of what such a suit will do to your reputation. Ensure food safety is a part of your culture and you won't have any issues with the health inspector.

Train Staff

Make sure all of your staff is properly trained. This is necessary because everyone who works at a food handling facility needs to have proper instruction in best practices. Health inspectors will question staff during their inspections and if anyone shows ignorance of food safety practices, you could be hit with a violation. Make sure everyone on your staff understands the importance of food safety.

If you make it a point of work culture, your staff will follow suit. If you display laxity towards it, and treat it as a hurdle to jump or just an issue to outmaneuver, you're building a time bomb that will only lead you to trouble.

Wash

Food handling is a delicate operation. Touch a single spoiled food item and your entire kitchen can get infected. This is why it's critical for you to regularly wash your hands and change gloves. Be very careful to separate the food handling and money accepting functions in your business. Accepting money and handling food immediately after can expose your customers to food poisoning.

With the advent of digital payments, this problem is decreasing but you need to be very conscious of how you're handling these processes. Do not let the person handling food anywhere near the cash box when you're open. If you're the one handling cash and are passing food onto your customers, make sure the food is properly packed so that there's no contact with your hands.

Clean Produce

Produce, even locally sourced, travels a long way from farms to the kitchen. It's stored with food from other farms and is mixed with food of varying quality. They're transported in trucks of varying hygienic levels and by the time it reaches your kitchen, there's no telling where it's been.

It's prudent to wash all produce thoroughly. You can even purchase a special vegetable wash that removes all contaminants from the surface of the food. Ensuring that your produce is fresh is one thing. You need to make sure it's clean as well.

Proper Storage

It's easy to chuck things into the fridge and forget about them. Your storage practices need to be on point, and everything that you store in your freezer or fridge has to be labeled so that you know how fresh everything is. You will not sell out of food every day; so it's critical for you to make sure all of your food is appropriately stored and that you know how long their shelf life is.

Check the temperature of your fridge to make sure it's below 40°F. Temperatures higher than this lead to bacterial growth that can cause food poisoning.

Sanitize

Everything that touches food must be sanitized before and after it touches food. Utensils, countertops, cutting boards, and even human hands need to be cleaned thoroughly before touching food. This is common sense but it can be easy to forget to do this in the rush of service. Establish clear policies that will ensure your employees will follow them at all times.

Inspect Supplies

Inspect your supplies thoroughly so that you're not buying less than ideal products from your dealers. As I mentioned earlier, food travels a great distance before it arrives at your kitchen, so make sure it isn't contaminated before it gets there.

What Inspectors Look For

With the preceding practices in place, you'll be in a great position to satisfy even the most fastidious of inspectors. There are a few key practices that every inspector evaluates in an examination. Here they are in no particular order.

Handwashing

Contaminated hands are the biggest source of food poisoning in kitchens and it makes sense for inspectors to look for problems here. Make sure you and your employees always wash hands after touching unsensitized objects before touching food. A lot of this is common sense. Take care to cook vegan and meat dishes separately within your kitchen.

If you're advertising vegan options, you can't cook that food on the same surfaces or with the same utensils on which meat and animal products have been cooked. This isn't vegan food, after all. Your customers might not spot it but it's unlikely to pass the notice of a health inspector. Also, it's disrespectful to your customers to cook food in this manner. If it's a problem for you, don't serve vegan food. It's better than lying to them.

When you switch between handling produce and meat, make sure every surface is cleaned and sanitized. While cooking heat and deep cold kills most bacteria in meat, you can't be too careful. Analysis of food safety instructions regularly so that your employees are up to speed.

Approved Sources of Food

A particular area of concern are your suppliers. While you need to follow correct food safety practices, your suppliers need to do so as well. Inspectors are extremely sensitive about the permits and licenses of your suppliers. If they're not a recognized vendor of food or aren't certified to be handling food, you can expect penalties to rain down on them and you.

Storage Temperatures

Inspectors will take a look at the temperatures of your food storage facilities. Make sure you inspect your fridges regularly to ensure there aren't any malfunctions. You'll be busy with the processes central to your business, so make sure you're not ignoring any issues with regards to food safety. Make sure all electronic storage facilities are routinely maintained and are cleaned.

Cross-Contamination

Don't ever mix raw and cooked food together. This is a basic food hygiene practice but it's very easy to ignore it in the heat of the kitchen. You'll risk cross-contamination by mixing them together. Designate appropriate areas in your kitchen and within your truck where raw and cooked food needs to be handled.

These four items are the most critical things they'll look at. There are a number of other points that health inspectors will verify. While these aren't as critical, this doesn't mean they aren't as important.

Labeling

One of the keys to ensuring proper food safety is good labeling practices. All of your stored food needs to be labeled with the date it was cooked or bought. Write down the date and month on every container. Make sure you're sanitizing storage containers properly once they've been used.

Labeling also extends to your storage facilities themselves. Raw food needs to be stored away from cooked food. You can store them within the same fridge, but they need to be packed appropriately. Use your common sense here. Don't make the mistake of throwing everything together without labels or adequate packing into the same storage facility.

Permits

Yup, we're back to permits once more. They're a pain to research; applying for them takes time; and every government official is interested in them. While they're tangentially related to food safety, they are a part of doing business legally. Make sure all of your permits have been renewed and are up to date. You don't want to risk being shut down over an expired permit.

Instruments

Food trucks routinely use meat thermometers to make sure their food is properly cooked. A common cause of food poisoning is undercooking meat and poultry. Make sure your thermometers are working well and that you have backups. It's a good idea to use two thermometers to make sure everything is in working order. Food inspectors will verify temperature readings with instruments of their own, so be prepared for this.

Cleanliness

Cleanliness isn't so much an inspection item as much as it is a state of being. Everything in your truck and kitchen should be spotless. You need to clean each instrument and space after service, every time your kitchen is used. Many food business owners neglect cleaning since it's difficult to do. You've spent an entire day cooking food and the end of service brings a sigh of relief. You'll be tempted to relax and call it a day.

However, drill it into yourself and your staff that the day is not finished until every surface of your kitchen is cleaned and the trash has been disposed of. You don't need to clean the exterior of your truck every day, but as far as food handling surfaces, countertops, and utensils go, they have to be cleaned. Take care to clean the floors and the ceilings as well.

Grease often collects in these areas and as it builds up, dirt sticks to the surfaces. Cleaning these surfaces every night will ensure you avoid problems. If you're using ovens, friers, and other cooking pots, clean them every night with boiling water. Friers are especially critical since old grease collects in them. Many trucks use flat grills to cook food. Over time, a layer of carbonized food collects on top of them and will begin to coat all the food you cook. Scrape and clean such surfaces after service.

Cleanliness also extends to your personal hygiene. Make sure your hair is tied and that you're wearing hair nets when serving food. Have your employees worn gloves when serving food. If wearing gloves is impractical, they need to have clean nails, and they need to wash their hands regularly. Do not allow sick employees into your kitchen since they'll end up infecting everyone. The food industry is particularly bad with this but, thankfully, this attitude is changing.

Don't show up to work if you're sick as well. You might lose income during the days you're sick but it's better to rest and return healthy rather than push yourself and churn out substandard food. The difference will be tested by your customers and you could also end up infecting them with whatever you're carrying.

Chapter 13. Insider's Tips on How to Plan a Menu for Your Food Truck

Who are your customers? Identify your target customers. How to know your market? What are the best products?

Plan Your Menu

In order to plan the perfect menu, you should ask yourself some questions that will make the business of choosing which foods should go on the menu easy for you. Here are some of those questions:

1. What's easy for you to cook? Can you cook hotdogs without burning either side? Can you flip pancakes like a pro? Do you know how to make delicious patties with just the right number of condiments? You have to determine what you can cook so you can narrow your choices down instead of overwhelming yourself with the thought that you should cook every dish in the world.

2. What's your specialty? Of course, there are a couple of dishes that you know how to cook and that's exactly why you're planning to open a food truck business. But there will always be a dish that you're confident about and you know you can cook better than anyone else does. What is it? Think about it and think about how you can use it for this business. For example, you can cook Fettuccine Alfredo like you're from Italy and you know that it tastes

different from what others make. Think about that and see if you can make more variations, or if you want to feature this food with some side dishes. This way, when people think about your food truck, they'll remember your specialty dish and they'd keep coming back for more.

3. Which ingredients are easily available around you? Maybe you're planning to put up a hotdog food truck but you're in an area where there are loads of fish and fresh produce around. What do you do? Will you still get meat for the hotdog from another town, or will you make use of the ingredients close to you, especially if you can actually make great dishes out of them? Sometimes, it's important to look around and see what you can do with what you have around because that will save you a lot of money, and may even make you closer to people around you, as well!

4. What do people who are routinely in the area where you would like to operate like to eat? Or, what are they looking for? Get to know your customers. Of course, it may be impossible to meet each and every one of them but it wouldn't be impossible to observe and make a general assessment as to what kind of food they enjoy the most. This way, when you set up your food truck, you can be sure that at least one or two people will try what you have to offer. On the other hand, you can also observe what's lacking in the area and you can check whether you can give them that or not. For example, New York is full of these pizza, pretzel, and hotdog kiosks, and food trucks. However, there's a lack of sushi trucks or even trucks that sell ramen or maybe even something organic. You can cook

and offer people lots of dishes, so research on that. If you offer people what they're missing or what's not currently available in the area, you just might get a positive response because more often than not, people want to try what they still haven't before.

5. What types of food can clients easily bring with them? As a customer, it's important to know that you'll be able to eat something easy to bring, especially because most people are on the go these days. So, it's essential that you make the packaging of your products efficient so that people won't have a hard time with them.

6. Which ingredients are too costly? Think about the dishes that you'll be making and see to it that you're not wasting too much money on ingredients, especially if you don't have enough budget, to begin with. Think about a dish that you can make and you know you're good at, that won't cost too much. It's important not to waste a lot of money when you're only starting.

7. Which ingredients are portable? There may be times when you lack ingredients in the truck and you have to buy some more from the nearest store, but what if it's a couple of miles away? You have to think about the ingredients that you'll be using, too, because they're important when it comes to the dishes that you'll be cooking.

8. Which food products are easy to re-heat? If you're planning to set up an Industrial Catering Vehicle, it would be important to know which food products you can easily re-heat without them losing their quality, and you have to

learn which foods don't get spoiled easily, as well, as you'll be traveling around a lot.

9. Are you going to focus on your expertise or willing to try something new? Suppose you're famous for creating delicious and appetizing cupcakes. Are you going to sell them or make them the focus of your business? Or are you also willing to learn how to make other dishes and make use of them, too? Differentiation is really important we're talking about food trucks, but being confident with what you're doing is as well one of the greatest keys to success.

10. Will your menu always be your menu, or will you be able to change it? It's important to observe whether your customers like your menu or not, and be open to changes if needed.

11. What time will you be open and on which days? You have to create a schedule and you have to stick to it because when your customers notice that you're not around for a day or two, or when they notice you're not open at a certain given time, they may think that you're no longer in business, or that you're not serious with what you're doing. That's definitely something that you shouldn't allow to happen.

When you are decided on what kind of menu you will offer your customers, you have to take care that you get to cook the food properly.

Also, you must think about some rules that will help your customers create the perfect food truck dish. Among these rules, the main ones are:

1. You must make sure you are consistent. Consistent in what? you may be asking. Well, consistent when it comes to making good food. Remember that you're not planning to have people eat at your place and never come back anymore, right? Therefore, you need to be sure that you always get to create good food so when they recommend you to other people, they won't be embarrassed that they did so and you'd gain more customers, too.

2. Make food that you won't have a tough time serving. Food trucks are mainly created for people who are on the go, so you have to learn how to work fast but still make sure that what you're doing is right. Create dishes that are easy to serve so people won't be bored and there won't be much pressure on you.

3. And, make food that remains good even if it's taken on the road. You have to expect that your customers will take their orders with them on the go. Of course, some people may stay at your food truck and eat but most of the customers may choose to just take their orders with them. Take care of the packaging and make sure to use only the right kinds of ingredients.

Pricing Your Menu

Pricing your menu properly can be scary, especially if you have never sold anything. Assigning a fair value to products can be difficult for some people.

Make prices too low, and you may be quite busy but have *little to show for it.*

Go too high and no one stops to eat. In pricing, you have to be Goldilocks, finding that 'just right' balance of price vs. value.

Value goes beyond high-quality products on your menu. Value is perceived in the delivery of the said menu. A clean cart or trailer, fantastic service, witty interaction with your guests, and a location convenience, all contribute in adding value to your products.

How many times have you groaned at the price of toilet paper at a convenience store only to buy it anyway because it saved you time? Your location provides a food choice for your guests plus saving them time, gasoline, and trouble.

I often work on the beach, so my base pricing is higher than other areas in the USA. I once set up 5 days a week at a very remote subdivision being built by a developer that had 100 to 150 workers. It was located an hour inland and 20 minutes from the nearest town. The closest and the only food was pizza, with limited toppings, made in an old dirty Exxon station with 2 gas pumps (the kind that dinged every gallon!).

I set up my shop in the middle of the subdivision construction and used my higher beach pricing without a problem. By the end of the construction, nearly the entire group of workers was eating with me. This was one such scenario where I actually did work about 3 hours a day from prep to service to clean up. Because the entire site shut down at once for lunch, the workers had enough time to eat; so I needed help handling the crowd.

Pro Tip: Location Convenience Adds a Significant Value in Justifying Higher Prices

When I price my food, I include everything that a guest could possibly want on the product that I would not upcharge them for. Then I look at different price points and ask, 'Would I pay that amount, and is that price comparable to the competition?'

Pro Tip: You Don't Have to Be Cheaper to Be Perceived as Better

The hamburger example cost us $1.44 and could sell for $5.75, giving a 25.04% food cost. It was fully dressed in common condiments.

$6.00 is a quite common (which we are under) street price for a ¼ lbs. burger. What if another area would not pay that and I had to drop it to $5.00 to stay competitive? No problem, food cost is still a great 28.80%.

How about an economically depressed area and you had to match a Wendy's single pricing? The average price of a single cheese is $4.19 at Wendy's. Using that price, our food cost would be

34.37%, and that puts us in the danger zone for profitability. Don't panic or throw in the towel.

Pro Tip: Bundle High Food Cost Items with Low-Cost Sides and Drinks to Lower the Overall Food Cost, and Increase the Ticket Averages

This increases the perceived value of the purchase and leaves the guest feeling like they got a good deal. Best of all it lowers the overall food cost and the impact of the fixed costs on your bottom line.

Chapter 14. Food Truck Vs Restaurants

The humble food truck is now a ubiquitous sight in many cities and towns across North America. It's very common to find a lineup of these interesting vehicles parked along the street on any given day.

Because food trucks are more economical to purchase and operate than brick-and-mortar restaurants, they appeal to many aspiring restaurant owners. More food truck-friendly states (at least in the US) often have laws that support mobile food businesses. In states where these businesses are legally protected, you can make more money than if you had a restaurant location— but you will also be working much harder.

The lower overhead associated with operating a food truck, coupled with the variety of menu choices offered by vendors, has made it an attractive option for people who wish to enter the restaurant business.

Let us now analyze which is better: food truck or restaurant:

One of the initial expenses faced by prospective owners is the cost of purchasing their mobile food business. Food trucks can be purchased new or used, and many websites feature listings of sellers advertising their vehicles for sale. You can also consider hiring a truck leasing company that will allow you to drive a truck that is already up-and-running.

While restaurants' cost of entry is much higher, food trucks typically purchase a smaller vehicle with smaller cooking facilities. This enables entrepreneurs to minimize startup costs and keep their overhead low. The learning curve for getting a food business up-and-running is considerably shorter with a truck versus a restaurant.

The practicality of food trucks cannot be ignored. Below you can find some reasons why they might be more profitable than restaurants:

- An attractive option for people who want to go into business for themselves but don't have the capital required to purchase or lease an existing restaurant location.
- Trucks can go almost anywhere, offering a wider range of consumers than if you had a brick-and-mortar location.
- Unlike restaurants, food trucks run on propane or natural gas, thus eliminating the need to pay for electricity.
- Food trucks are mobile, so a prospective entrepreneur doesn't have to worry about finding a location with lots of foot traffic for their business.
- Lower operating costs mean greater profits. For example, using propane or natural gas as your primary fuel source will save you money and help you keep prices down on your menu offerings. The ability to offer affordable meals is an aspect that some consumers appreciate about food trucks.

Creating a food truck business is relatively easy from a legal standpoint, but you have to capitalize on your marketing skills and be creative with your business plan. Consider the following:

- Keep your overhead as low as possible.
- Understand that truck drivers are not employees—they're independent contractors. This means you don't have to pay payroll taxes, but you also don't get employer-matching contributions for their health care and other benefits.
- Check local laws and ordinances about where food trucks can be parked while serving their customers.

If your desire is to open a restaurant, there is no reason why you should forego the idea due to financial limitations. Consider the following comparisons of food trucks and restaurants:

- You can lease space from a property owner, as opposed to buying a truck. Leasing gives you more flexibility if your business isn't doing well.
- Restaurant owners are not subject to additional taxes and fees that apply to independent contractors.
- As a restaurant owner, you can schedule employees as needed—they don't have to be on-call like food truck workers do.

Chapter 15. Reasons Why You Should Integrate a Food Truck into Your Food Business

The food truck industry is one of the fastest-growing industries in the US. There are lots of reasons for you to integrate a food truck into your food business. Let us enumerate it:

Fast Start-Up

When integrating a food truck into your restaurant, the start-up is usually faster compared to the old-fashioned way of starting your shop. Today, food trucks are available for rent by the day and you can find a food truck vendor that is willing to lease a truck to you. If you need more trucks for service, you can add more units at lesser cost compared to opening a new restaurant from scratch.

Competitive Eating

If your first plan is to compete with other restaurants in your area, then a food truck can certainly be a good solution for you, (probably the best one) as it has the ability to stay competitive in crowded areas. A food truck will certainly provide a unique selling point and differentiates itself from others by being able to provide quick and accessible services, especially during peak hours.

Low Budget Operation

Operating a food truck is very flexible and it doesn't need a lot of investment. Compared to restaurants, the initial cost for food trucks and their maintenance are usually minimal. This is especially advantageous if you're a newbie in the business, as your financial risk will be limited.

High Mobility

The key to making profits in this business is to "be where your customers are" therefore, high mobility of your business is crucial. Unlike restaurants that have heavy equipment and slow service, a food truck can deliver service much quicker. It can also be relocated as needed depending on the business' demand. Since most food trucks are driven, it enables more hands-on approach to the business, especially if you plan to drive your own truck.

Mobile Branding

A food truck can be a great tool to promote your brand. If you are able to attract potential customers of your business through your food truck, chances are that they'll know about your other ventures and go back there someday soon. Food trucks are great for advertising because of their mobility and ability to attract a crowd. In fact, adding a mobile kitchen in front of any business will immediately increase foot traffic in businesses located nearby.

Lack of Required Ingredients

If you're tired of buying fresh ingredients and still not being able to generate profit, this is the best solution for you. Because of its simplicity and convenience, people may want to have a bite from your food truck. Food trucks can be served at any location and it doesn't need a lot of ingredients to be cooked, unlike restaurants that need a lot of ingredients for their daily business operations.

Small Investment

When it comes to opening up a food truck business, you'll be surprised by how cheap it is. This type of food business can start out as low as $20,000 to $30,000 and can grow even without having an initial large capital investment. It also requires less work in terms of employees than most restaurants.

A Higher Profit Margin than Eating Establishments that Cook In-House

This could be one of the reasons why you should make a food truck into your business. According to recent studies, sales volume and revenue per truck are about 20% higher compared to that of restaurants. The biggest reason is that food trucks already have a built-in customer base and many customers already visit them regularly.

High-Profit Margin Selling Savory Snacks

Food trucks that sell savory snacks usually earn higher profit margins compared to those selling sweet items like cake or pastry because they require less labor and simple preparation techniques. For instance, if you're targeting hungry people, you can only focus on selling snacks that can give quick satisfaction or those who want a casual meal such as hot dogs, burgers, and sandwiches etc.

Great Source of Revenue During the First Three Months

According to many food trucks owners, the first three months of business is usually very profitable for them, provided they can build their reputation in the community. Food trucks have high turnover rate and many customers visit them often. This is especially why you should try a food truck as a business.

No Need to Worry about Permits, Building Permits, or Opening a Bank Account

Unlike restaurants, food trucks don't need to worry about permits or building permits because they usually last a short period of time. If you want to change locations fast without the hassle of processing paperwork, this is especially advantageous.

High-Profit Margin Despite Low Prices

Food trucks can sell at a higher price compared to restaurants that offer the same menu because customers value variety and taste.

Flavors and Freshness

For your chance to have a unique menu and build a reputation for your business, food trucks offer you creative freedom, especially when it comes to stand-out menu items and flavor combinations. You can also use fresh ingredients in making your food in order to make it more appealing in terms of flavor and presentation.

Besides Catering and Restaurant Business, Food Trucks Are Also Selling Their Products at Pop-Ups and Events

A great way to test your ideas, food and brand is by using pop-ups. It's a relatively low-cost way of getting your food out there without dedicating to a location. Pop-ups are also great for testing out the market. And if you're at a retail show or another event that is part of an expo, this can also be great for you to display your products. So, there you have it—seven reasons why you should enter the food truck business.

Chapter 16. Specialized Insurances for Food Trucks and Street Food Vendors

Food Truck Insurance

We need to preface this part with the following disclaimer: We are not insurance agents and you cannot consider this information as an official legal advice. You should consult with an insurance professional when it comes to insuring your business and protecting your assets.

While you may well be on your way to building a great food truck, there's one more part of the equation that needs to be addressed when it comes to your vehicle and business. That's where insurance comes in. Whenever customers do business with you, there's always the risk that something could go wrong. Common incidents, like bodily injury or property damage can happen at any time and you need to be protected from expenses and claims that could arise suddenly.

No one is able to say when an accident will happen but even small claims could put your business in a dire situation. Claims can also come from your employees from accidents that occur on the job. But you need to realize that accidents don't just happen in the kitchen. Simply driving your truck from one location to another opens up many possibilities for misfortunes from you or other drivers on the road. And don't forget that your truck can even be stolen, which could put you out of commission for days/weeks, or be completely devastating for your business.

When shopping for insurance for your food truck, make sure the insurance company understands the needs of mobile food trucks and their owners. The food truck industry is just a small segment of the food and beverage industry and you need to be sure the provider you choose can offer the coverage you need. Some of the services you should ask about are:

- General Liability
- Commercial Auto Liability
- Operations Coverage
- Products Coverage
- Damage to Premises
- Personal Property Coverage
- Business Property Coverage
- Cyber Liability Insurance
- Workers' Compensation
- Unemployment Insurance
- Umbrella Coverage (Excess Liability)

The insurance companies will also perform checks on the persons who will be driving the food truck. These come in the form of Motor Vehicle Reports. Drivers you employ who fall into a particular risk profile will result in higher premiums for your business. It's possible that the insurance provider may choose not to cover your business at all because of risky drivers on your payroll. So, before you apply for insurance, check the driving records of your drivers to see how many moving violations or accidents (if any) they've had in the last 36 months.

Additional Insurance Requirements

If you plan on doing business at various venues and events, you may need to prove that you are insured before you are even allowed on the property. This is typically called an Additional Insured Certificate. This can include venues like food truck pods, festivals, private locations and more. Most venues require that your policy includes at least $1 million General Liability coverage. This protects the venue or event from accidents caused by your business activities on their premises. Each certificate can cost $25 to $100 or more. If you attend many events during a year, these expenses can add up quickly. But definitely ask upfront whether an insurance provider requires fees for these certificates. There are some insurance companies that won't charge you extra for this service.

Do your research in this area and get advice from an insurance professional. Since food trucks consist of only a small portion of the food and beverage industry, some insurance companies may not be familiar with the specific policies or requirements for food trucks. Make sure you ask a lot of questions and find out if they are familiar with the food truck industry and the needs of food truck owners. Similar to consulting with a medical doctor, it's worth getting second and third opinions on this subject to make sure you're protected!

Chapter 17. Customer Service

Getting new customers is the way you grow your business. It's no wonder that businesses exert a lot of time and money to bring in new customers. According to studies, it costs 5 to 10 times more to acquire a new customer than it does to sell to a loyal existing customer. There's also research that reveals that existing customers spend 67% more than new customers. So, you can see that keeping customers coming back is extremely beneficial to your food truck business. The mobile food industry is very competitive; you need to attract and keep customers buying from you and not your competitors.

What can you do to keep your customers coming back and spending their money in your business? The answer is with a customer loyalty program. A good portion of businesses has implemented some sort of customer loyalty or rewards program to entice customers to come back and buy.

Loyalty programs work the best with businesses that serve constant customers. Restaurants and food trucks fall into that category. If you have amazing food and great customer service, you will get your clients coming back. To keep them returning, reward them for their continued patronage. Have you ever been to a restaurant to get that 11th sandwich for free?

Effective Loyalty Programs

You've probably seen a loyalty program in many businesses you've visited. But a loyalty program is simply a rewards program that companies offer to customers that make frequent purchases. This loyalty program rewards customers who keep coming back with special offers, gifts, free merchandise, coupons, and more!

While loyalty programs seem like it's simple to implement, let me throw out the following facts. A recent study has shown that a given household typically has memberships to 29 loyalty programs. However, out of all those they have signed up for, they are really engaged only in about 12 of them. That means a lot of companies are spending a lot of time and money on rewards programs but seeing very little to no benefit from them. The key is to offer value to your customers for being a part of your loyalty program. So how do you increase your ability to make loyalty programs be more effective for your food truck business?

Loyalty Program Features

Loyalty programs are offered by many companies and the choices can be overwhelming. Some are simple, while others are feature-rich and advanced. It's important to pick one that you think will work with your food truck business for the long term. However, you can never tell if these loyalty programs will close shop or be acquired by a larger rewards program. But fear can't stop you from implementing a loyalty program.

I will give you some ideas and suggestions when searching for a loyalty program that is right for you. Use this as a guide so you can be better informed before you implement a system for your food truck. It is not strange to switch programs if over time you find that it is not working for you. Here are some suggestions and features to consider.

Simple Point Systems

One of the most common and oldest loyalty program systems is the point system. Customers that visit your food truck frequently can accumulate points that can be exchanged for rewards once they've reached the threshold you've set. They can receive a discount, free items, or even special treatment and more!

You've seen these before and can come in many forms. Some are simple punch cards, while others use magnetic cards and a database to keep track of points. The point system should be simple to understand. Don't over-complicate this! The term points can refer to various tracking methods. For example:

- Buy 10 sandwiches get the 11th free
- Spend $50 get your next dish free

The point system encourages frequent short-term purchases that keep customers coming back, accruing points, and eventually getting rewarded for their continued visits to your food truck. You can assign points by the number of items or by the dollar amount spent.

Tier System

There is a tricky balance between a loyalty program and offering attainable and desirable rewards. You don't want to create a huge process for customers to reach reward thresholds. That will turn off your customers and your loyalty system become ineffective. One way to breach this problem is to use a tier system.

With a tier system, you can offer a reward for initially joining your loyalty program. This encourages sign-ups. Then you can bring back returning customers by increasing the value of the rewards you offer in different tiers. Each tier is made more attractive by offering higher value or better rewards as they move up the ladder. This can help customers remember your loyalty program because it encourages decreasing the time it takes for them to redeem their rewards. If the time between payouts for the reward is too long, customers will forget or ignore the loyalty program. The biggest difference between a points system and a tier system is that customers receive their rewards in the short-term.

So, with your food truck business, you can offer a free appetizer or drink for the initial sign-up to your loyalty program. Then after that, you can offer larger and larger rewards such as 2 appetizers free when they reach the next tier and then offer something else in subsequent tiers.

How to Measure Effectiveness

Just because you've implemented your loyalty program doesn't mean you're done! You need to be able to measure the success of your efforts. The goal of your loyalty program is to increase your customer's satisfaction and keep them coming back.

In today's business world, you will most likely be using a rewards program with an online database. These systems offer excellent tracking and analytics. A punch card system can work but it will be much more difficult to evaluate its effectiveness.

Customer Retention Rate

When evaluating your analytics, you want to first look at your Customer Retention Rate. This is a metric about how long your customers continue to buy from you. If your loyalty program is successful, this number should increase over time as you continue to add people to your program. Studies have shown that even a 5% increase in customer retention can translate to a 25% to 100% increase in your company's profits.

Negative Churn

You may or may not actually heard the term churn. But churn is the rate that your customers stop doing business with you. When I say negative churn, it indicates the rate at which customers increase spending with you. Negative churn helps to balance out the natural occurrence where customers leave your business.

Net Promoter Score

The net promoter score results from customer satisfaction and how likely they are to recommend your business to others. This is usually on a scale of 1 to 10 with 10 being the highest. The net promoter score is determined by looking at the percentage of detractors (people who wouldn't promote your business) and subtracting it from the number of promoters (people who would recommend your business).

The fewer detractors you have the better. You can consider a net promoter score of 70% and higher a good number. Promoting a great loyalty program you could reach that number. To get the satisfaction rating, you will have to send out surveys to customers. These are usually based online and can be sent as notifications via your chosen loyalty program.

When to Implement a Loyalty Program?

Loyalty programs can be implemented at any time during your business. For some older businesses, they've been doing business for years before starting a loyalty program. That could be because reliable systems weren't available when they started and now, they're realizing the benefits of having it.

Others start a loyalty program from the beginning or early on. But here's a suggestion. If you haven't launched your food truck yet, get on board with a loyalty company that fits your business. Have it in place before you launch. Then when you launch your truck, you can start customers on your loyalty program right from the start. Hold a special event when you launch and make sure you let customers know about the program.

You will find below a brief list to help you get started. These companies can come and go so by the time you read this, some of them can be or no longer be in business.

- Belly
- Square
- LevelUp
- FiveStars
- Wali
- Perka
- SpotOn
- PunchCard
- SpendGo
- Swipley
- FourSquare

Most if not all the rewards systems listed above utilize mobile apps and digital tracking to make it easier for your customers to keep track of their status. This helps clients know when they are close to receiving a reward and could entice them to come back for a visit.

Choosing Rewards for Customers

The kind of rewards offered to customers varies depending on the type of business. But there are some general rules to follow that increase the chances of a positive reward experience for your customers. Experts advise expanding your thinking from only offering discounts on your goods. That's because the discounts don't have a long-lasting impact on customer's impressions.

Rewards that have physical items are received and remembered much better than a plain discount. Luckily in the food truck industry, we can talk straight to customer's stomachs!

A good way to tailor your own rewards program is to imitate larger successful programs from related companies and offering something unique. You can research brick-and-mortar restaurants, bakeries, ice cream shops, food trucks, and more to see what they are doing. Sign-up for their programs so you can see first-hand how theirs works and to see the types of rewards they offer. Ask yourself if they seem reasonable and if their rewards are something that would even interest you.

Put together a program that offers the best of what you've seen and experienced. Another factor that determines how your rewards program works are tied directly to the service that you sign-up for. Some have more features than others. You may or may not need certain features. Price and fees will also be a factor. Remove those that don't fit your budget or have features you don't need or will never use. In the end, your customers want to be able to reap the rewards. It is ideal for them to be able to redeem an award about every 3 to 6 months so they don't forget about it. This will help stimulate them to come back and buy. A loyalty program should not take too long for a customer to see the results of their continued business with you. Otherwise, they will see no value in it.

It's a well-known fact that loyalty programs are a very effective marketing tool. When successfully implemented, they can help increase profits and keep customers coming back for more.

Loyalty programs can also help boost your brand awareness and ultimately your reputation. If you haven't done so, start researching the different loyalty programs available and plan out how you would implement them into your business. You wouldn't like to miss out on an excellent marketing opportunity that can result in a lot of positive advantages for your food truck!

Chapter 18. From Business Owner to Employer

Operating a food truck takes a big time commitment! Food truck owners start their day long before their first service starts. The day often begins with ingredient shopping, food preparation, social media updates, mechanical inspections and more. The end of the working day is also made up of work that could extend several hours after the last customer is served. This allows limited time for everything else. If the number of hours sounds overwhelming then it is time to hire additional help. In the beginning you may be doing everything yourself. And depending on the level of complexity of your food truck business, you may or may not need to hire additional hands to help out with daily operations. Many trucks operate with just the owners while just as many if not more have additional crew members helping with various tasks. The owners may even run one service at a location themselves and then have staff members in charge at a different location during the day.

There is definitely a benefit to having employees on your staff. The extra expense can be worth it so you don't burn yourself out. One of the first things you should consider is how many hours of work are required each day. As said before, you have to consider the hours of work prior to and after your actual service hours. For example, if you are open for business from 10am to 6pm, that equates to about a 60-hour workweek if you are open 7 days a week. That's not including the time spent before and after you open for business. If you add a minimum of 2 hours before and after your service hours, you're looking at almost 85 hours of work each week. That's more than twice the number of hours most people work at a regular job!

Add to those times any additional hours where you might stay open later or attend special events like catering parties and your workweek really starts to get over the top with the number of hours you need to put in. It could be that you only need additional help during these special events. Larger services like events and catering requires more preparation time and extra hands during the event. You will also be spending time meeting with your clients and venue representative as you map out your game plan for a successful event.

Some food trucks can operate with as little as 2 people on board and still handle a large volume of customers; but that depends on your menu. If your menu features foods that are simple to prepare, then a couple of people can probably manage the volume. Gourmet ice cream, donut and grilled cheese trucks for example can be well-suited for smaller staff operations. At minimum, you will need someone who can cook and someone who can take orders plus other side duties.

How Much of Your Time Is Required?

There's nothing wrong with long hours and hard work but there comes a point when it stops being fun. You have to decide how many hours you actually want to spend in the truck or doing other business-related tasks. This is when you need to determine the types of tasks you want to do most or have the most expertise in.

Do you enjoy cooking or talking to customers? Do you thrive with the backend business and marketing part of your operations? It's good to be aware of the tasks that is better spent with your own time and hiring employees to complete the work that can easily be done by others. That way, you can spend more time building your business than running daily operations. There's a big distinction between working in your truck and working on your food truck business.

What tasks can help you make the most revenue for your mobile food business? Your time might be better spent meeting with clients and booking special events, like catering rather than preparing food inside the kitchen.

You Don't Necessarily Need Full-Time Employees

Sometimes food truck owners can handle the workweek on their own without additional staff. But there are moments when taking on additional help can make your operations smoother. If you know there is an event or service where you know an exceptional volume of customers will be attending, then you can just hire temporary help during those events.

The good thing is that the people you hire don't obligatorily need experience in the food or restaurant industry. They can all be taught on the job as they work their way up to higher positions. Of course, experience working in a fast-paced environment and food service does help.

Job Duties for Your Employees

While there is probably not necessarily one specific job that an employee will be asked to do, I'll leave you with a selection of tasks you could ask your new hire to perform. The work varies and everyone has to help out in some way to ensure that the operations go smoothly during a service.

Depending on experience, a new hire will typically start as an order taker. Greeting customers and sending orders through to the kitchen is a job most people can do. This is often the best way to train new employees so they can get familiar with the workflow of your truck. From there, an employee can move to the prep table, where sauces and other finishing touches are added to dishes before they are handed to the customer.

The job that really dictates the workflow of the truck is the chef or person in charge of actually cooking the food. That could be the person working on a grill, fryer, crepe iron, or other piece of equipment. Order tickets go to the chef, where the whole cooking and preparation process starts.

Key Role of the Chef

The efficiency of the whole operation rests on the hands of the chef or the person in charge of cooking and prepping the main food items. They are the ones that get the meats and vegetables prepped before service. They are the ones that monitor the orders coming in and pace the flow of the food heading out.

This person needs to be organized and be able to manage many things going on at one time. Different dishes require different prep times. This can be challenging even for the most experienced chef. Long lines and special requests can put added pressure on the one in charge of the kitchen.

Scheduling Employees and Pay Rates

Food truck employees aren't the highest-paid workers but it's a good way to earn some income or just extra cash. Typical starting pay for a food truck employee is $8.00 an hour. Once your employee gets more experience and moves into a cooking position, rates can be $10.00 or more. On top of that, your employees can enjoy a bit of extra tips generated from each service location.

One of the side benefits for your employees is that you could offer them free food at the end of each shift. If you're friends with other trucks, you might share meals between the other trucks at the end of a service. This is easy to do if you are grouped together, so workers and owners can bond and sample what everyone has to offer.

Food trucks typically operate 2 to 3 services a day. That means breakfast, lunch, and dinner. A service can last 3 to 6 hours depending on the location and type of event. Commonly, the time spent actually cooking and serving food will be about 3 to 4 hours. Don't forget the additional hours spent preparing for the service and clean up afterwards.

Some trucks can serve up to 150 orders or more per service. That means in a 4-hour service, food is ordered, cooked, and served to a customer every 90 seconds. Add to that, modified orders, customer complaints, and mixed-up orders; the work experience can be very hectic to say the least. So, it does help to hire employees that can handle these high-pressure situations.

Chapter 19. Building Your Brand

When building a memorable brand, it's important to use research to collect data on your area's target market. It's important to know the market and create a niche within that market.

Find out what you can offer that your competitors are unable to offer. Find out what your customers care about—price, quality, etc. Using this knowledge—you can be different and stand out within your crowd—delivering quality items that no one else can create!

In terms of marketing your food truck, being different means finding your "unique selling point." This means identifying what your business, and no one else, can offer. This usually comes from your unique experiences and skills. Create something exclusive to you and your business.

Another major area to work on is customer service; which can be closely tied to your brand. Nothing can destroy a brand quicker than poor customer service. It truly doesn't matter if your brand sells luxury items or potato chips, customer service is vital for success. If you don't manage your customers with respect, they won't be coming back.

Another brand-building technique is delivering your services in a memorable manner. Know what your customers are expecting and deliver above and beyond. Use social media to embrace loyal customers and sell or give away items with your logo attached.

Finally, deliver on any promises and take suggestions. When building a brand, provide trust to your customers and take advice seriously if it can enhance your business. Not every outside idea will be notable, but make sure to listen and make the right choices for your brand.

Naming Your Food Truck

Naming a food truck can be difficult. More often than not, puns are involved because it's important to create a memorable name to bring in customers. These puns can come from pop culture, music, local sayings, or historic literature.

For those hoping to avoid the pun game, consider using a catchy word along with a first or last name. Some catchy introductory words include **sweet, fresh, taco, fusion, cheesy, southern, speedy, mighty, danger,** or **curry.**

In addition, there are ending words as well, where a first name came be followed with BBQ pit, inferno, sliders, paradise, shack, heroes, wings, express, city, odyssey, blend, buns, mobile, funk, or on-wheels.

As with naming any business, be sure to check on trademarked names. There have been several stories in the news where a food truck owner innocently chose a name for their truck only to find someone suing them for using it. Like with other aspects of starting a food truck, researching and choosing your truck name should not be done quickly!

Commissaries and Commercial Kitchens

A very important and integral step in the formation of your food truck business is finding a commissary where your food truck can call home. Essentially, a commissary is like a commercial kitchen, meaning it is a commercially licensed unit for storing or cooking food.

Food trucks must have a commissary or commercial kitchen for parking. Some cities do not allow actual cooking to be performed on a truck, but even so, a commercial kitchen or commissary is absolutely crucial for preparation and food storage.

Much like your food truck living up to local health standards, so must a commercial kitchen. It's important to find a proper commercial kitchen, because if the one your truck uses is unlicensed for any reason (even temporarily), your truck will also be out of commission.

The size, location, and style of commissary or commercial kitchen will also dictate the cost and which types of dishes can be created within the kitchen. In order to find the ideal location for your needs, contact the ones in your area with the knowledge of your foods and the quantity that you will need to prepare on workdays.

There are shared and private commercial kitchens as well as restaurant kitchens. Shared are leased to several cooks while private leases are for individual businesses and perhaps the most ideal for food trucks. Restaurants' kitchens can also be useful on their off days if you can strike a deal with them. It's important to note that an actual facility named a "commissary" is not necessary but some sort of commercial kitchen is definitely required because of health standards. You cannot just park your food truck at home when it's not in use.

Chapter 20. Q&A Appendix

Here you can find some frequently asked questions about Food Truck Businesses:

Q. What are the benefits of buying a food truck?

A. With a food truck, you can make money by selling what you cook in your business, instead than working for somebody else and potentially not getting paid very well. You can also start your own business with minimal cash outlay. Another benefit is that the cost of starting a food truck is low compared to if you were opening up an actual restaurant location. A final benefit is that it's easy to find parking in a lot or on the side of the street as opposed to renting out space, which can cost several thousand dollars per month for rent alone.

Q. What is the distinction from a food truck and a mobile food business?

A. A food truck is a vehicle that you can use to cook and sell your meals. A mobile food business (not to be confused with a food truck) is any kind of vending mechanism, such as a pushcart or stand.

With the latter, all of the ingredients have to be pre-cooked or ready to eat (such as hotdogs on a cart). Whereas with a food truck, you can sell raw ingredients and cook them for customers right in front of them.

Q: Can I cook in a mobile food business?

A. Yes, you can cook anything you want in a mobile food business. But take into account they were not designed for it and the job will be difficult. This is the main difference between a mobile food business and a food truck, since you can cook on a truck.

Q: Can I still use my existing recipes and products at the fair?

A. Yes, but remember that most people like to eat something hearty when they are walking around outside in the cold! You should adapt your recipes so that they are quick and easy to eat with little mess.

Q: How do I find a food truck for sale for the right price?

A. When it comes to buying a food truck, the most important factor is usually the condition of the truck. Start by searching in your local newspaper classified ads and online listings (Craigslist, eBay, etc.). If you don't find any trucks that are in good condition at an affordable price, then contact a local food truck association (listed below) and ask for help. They will probably know other owners that might be selling their trucks since they talk to each other often.

Q: How expensive is to buy a food truck?

A. It really just depends on the truck, since there are no standard prices. You can buy a new food truck for $200,000 and up, or you can buy a used truck for $40,000 or less.

As a rough rule, you'll need to spend at least about $40,000 to make it worth it (with more depending on the cost of your menu).

Q: Where do I get a food truck permit?

A. You need to get a permit from the state government that oversees the city where you live. A unit of each state's website is dedicated to helping small businesses with these permits.

Chapter 21. Conclusion

The food truck business is a very lucrative industry that has drastically increased in popularity over the last few years. Many people want to get into this business in hopes of making a profit and having their own business. There are several different types of food trucks from which to choose, such as ice cream trucks, hot dog stands, or crepe carts. One person's trash is another person's treasure, and any type of food truck will be successful if you know what you're doing. Food trucks can be a lot of fun and very lucrative, but several things need to be taken into consideration before you jump right in. The first is the type of truck you're planning to invest in! Deciding which truck and set up is perfect for your food business will depend on many different factors.

Firstly, do you like the product? Have you ever been attracted to a food truck or seen one on the street and thought that's what I want my business to look like? If so, then that's a good place.

Secondly, how much capital do you have to invest into this food truck business? Some food trucks are more expensive than others and this will be your first big expense. When looking at food trucks, make sure that the price is reasonable and that you feel like you can afford it.

Thirdly, will this truck fit into the area that you live in? If you plan on selling crepes then a large truck isn't needed, but if you have dreams of selling hot dogs and hamburgers, then a large truck with a huge grill on top would be ideal. The size of your truck will affect what products you can sell because not all recipes fit onto all types of grills or ovens.

Always remember these tips about food truck businesses:

1. Start out small. As mentioned before, don't go out and buy the biggest food truck on the market. Start small and work your way up. This will let you see how much money will be made from this business venture.
2. Be creative with your menu! Don't sell the same things as another food truck that is on the street in your area because chances are, they're making more money than you because they're doing something different and people love it! Create your own business cards, logos, or slogan to differentiate yourself from all other food trucks in your area.
3. Get involved with your local community and spread the word about your business! This is so important for many reasons. You will gain customers by being involved, and it will be easier to create a niche for yourself in the food truck industry.
4. Plan it out. When thinking about opening up a food truck business you should do some market research and look into trends of what food trucks are selling the most in your area. Are there other trucks selling coffee? Iced tea? If so, it might be best to stay away from that product because someone else may be making more money than you on a product that's already been established in that area.

So, here's a basic overview of the elements that make up a food truck business. We've deliberated everything from logistics to finances and everything in between. However, as I hope you can see, many different factors go into determining if a food truck business is right for you. Be sure to give careful consideration to each point mentioned before deciding how to proceed with your endeavor. And remember that we are always happy to help!

Thank you for reading Food Truck Business!

If you enjoyed this book, I would be grateful if you could take a minute of your time to share it with me by leaving a review.

I think your opinion can help other people find the right solution to their problems, and helps me find new suggestions to offer you content that always fits your needs.

Kyle Locklear

Scan the QR code to leave a review

Made in the USA
Las Vegas, NV
15 September 2023